MADE IN JAPAN

PART I

To Grace
Sincerely

Lillian Natsue
Uehara Morgan

MADE IN JAPAN

LILLIAN NATSUE UEHARA MORGAN'S
LIFE STORY

Wakayama Castle

LILLIAN NATSUE UEHARA MORGAN

To order additional copies of this book, contact:
Xlibris Corporation
1-888-795-4274
www.Xlibris.com
Orders@Xlibris.com
95155

CONTENTS

About the Author

The author was a child born in Japan prior to WWII to an American missionary mother and a Japanese physician father. This book is a true account of her life from 1930 through the difficult and, at times, horrific war-torn years in Japan. She had to overcome racial prejudice because she was an *ainoko* (meaning "child of mixed marriage"). She earned U.S. citizenship in 1958 and continued a fulfilling life as a registered nurse until her retirement in 1990.

Preface

Here is to you, my grandchildren on the Yelton side of our family and your children to come. Maybe my life story would make a good bedtime story as my mother read a story to my younger sister and me each night. Anyone else who is interested is welcome to listen.

This is a true account of my life from my birth in 1930 in Japan, living through WWII, my arrival in the United States of America in 1950 to the completion of my college education in 1954.

My professional life (1954-1990) as a registered nurse was a very rewarding experience, and I have never once regretted serving the needs of others.

So here I am, at the ripe old age of eighty and before senile dementia catches up with me, I have decided to write this book.

As to my grandchildren on the Morgan side of the family, I came into your lives by marriage to your grandpa Donald Morgan. This book will give you a bird's-eye view of your grandma Lillian's childhood. Perhaps you can get to know me better.

Natsue Uehara, age five   Natsue Uehara in 1950

Acknowledgments

I would like to thank my husband, Donald E. Morgan, for his persistent encouragement and help in the computer skills in completing this book.

I want to express my sincere thanks to my friend Judie Gordon for spending many hours of her precious time reviewing my manuscript to complete the preliminary editing. Your interest and talent are much appreciated.

Introduction

This book is a true account of a child born in Japan prior to WWII to an American missionary mother and a Japanese physician father. She grew up during the difficult times of the war years, overcoming hunger, fear, and racial discrimination. This is a testimony of the resilience of human spirit, dedicated to her grandchildren so they might get to better know their grandmother.

My Birthday

It was a very hot and humid Sunday, August 10, 1930. My mother and father were attending Wakayama Presbyterian Church. As Mother was getting up from the church pew to sing a hymn, she felt the first faint contraction. She told my father they better start thinking about going home to get the baby clothes and then get on the interurban train leaving Higashi Wakayama eki (East Wakayama City Japan National Railroad Station).

I know this trip home from the church and back to the station took at least an hour. Then the Wakayama station to Tennoji Osaka station was an hour ride. Mother told me the pains were getting closer by the minute. By the time they arrived at the St. Barnabas Hospital at Tennoji Osaka, her pains were thirty minutes apart. Ms. Van Kirk, the head nurse, took one look at Mother and scolded her for not coming in sooner. Mother had lingered until the church service was over and had lunch before she and my father left Wakayama City. At least five hours had passed since her first backache.

Well, to make a long story short, I was born on August 10, 1930, at 8:00 p.m. Baby and mother (at age forty) both did well. Mother was fed American-style food and had lots of rest before she was allowed to return home.

St. Barnabas Hospital was an American Episcopalian Mission Hospital specializing in obstetrics and pediatric patient care. It was built by an American physician in 1873 and, at the time of my birth, staffed by some American physicians and American-trained nurses headed by Ms. Van Kirk. This hospital was also a school for training registered nurses and midwives. The scholastic standing of the school was very high.

St. Barnabas Hospital was miraculously spared by the bombing of Osaka City during WWII and did not perish. About 1980, I took time to return to the hospital and visited the original section of the buildings. I was greeted by the same hospital smell I remembered as a child. The staff had completely changed to all-Japanese physicians and nurses. They took me back to the record room. There I saw the book of records that announced my birth. I could make out my name, the only baby born on August 10, 1930, at this hospital. I was born under the zodiac sign of Leo during the year of the Horse according to the Chinese calendar.

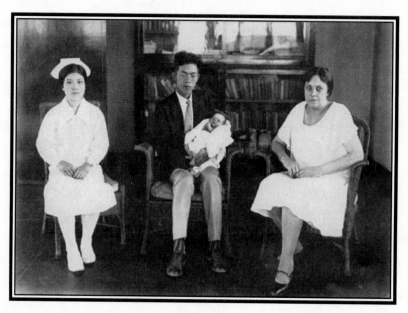

Nurse   My father, me   Ms. Van Kirk

How My Name Was Chosen

The naming of a child in Japan is a major task. Usually, the head of the household, the father of the child, or a grandfather selects the Chinese character appropriate to the family tradition: prosperity and good will toward the child. Because I was born in August, my father took the Chinese character Natsu (meaning "summer"). He did not particularly want to end my name with Ko ("child"), which was commonly used in naming a female child in Japan. After exhausting the list, my father opened the Christian Bible, in Japanese, closed his eyes and pointed to a word, *sakaeru* which meant "glory, prosperity." Thus he named me Natsue (meaning "summer glory").

Now I had a first name, Natsue, and last name, Uehara (meaning "upper field"). I was born on my mother's sister Lillian's birthday. Thus, when I was about to come to the United States, I needed another name to satisfy the space for a middle initial, so I took my aunt's name, Lillian, to be my first and my Japanese name Natsue as my middle name. It was easier for everyone to pronounce my first name, Lillian, rather than Natsue. Almost always, foreigners mispronounced my name Natsui, and often I had to correct the pronunciation.

How Mother Came to Japan
and Met My Father

I would like to tell you about my mother by starting out with some family history taken out of the Fulghum family archives. The following is a direct quote from the "Fulgham-Fulghum Family Facts," published in March 2004, page 7, written by Robert S. Fulghum (Lillian's first cousin).

Charles Mallary Fulghum was the ninth child of *James Fulghum* and *Jane (Harrison) Fulghum*. He was born 5 August 1860 in Washington County Georgia. Orphaned at age three, Charles was reared by the Nathanial Hooks family. He was married on 30 November 1887 in Sanderson, Georgia, to *Matilda (Slade) Fulghum* (born 21 March 1864 in Linton, Georgia, died 9 February 1955 in Macon, Georgia). Charles and Tillie had eight children: *May*, died soon after birth; *Sarah Frances (Fulghum) Uehara* (born 29 May 1890, died 17 February 1973); *Matilda*, died as an infant; *Lillian Winefred* (born 10 August 1894, died 1962); *Charles Mallary*, died as infant; *Nathanial*, died as infant; *James Hooks* (born 18 September 1905, died 1982); and *Charles Bennett* (born 23 November 1906, died 1976).

Charles Mallary Fulghum worked as a building contractor, wholesale and retail grocer, and merchant-broker in Macon, Georgia. He was a Baptist deacon in the Vineville Baptist Church of Macon. He also was an incessant student of the Bible. Self-educated and extremely well-read, he was on the executive council of Mercer University in Macon.

His children were brought up in a very religious home that provided a rather strict Baptist environment. Consequently, they excelled in their work. A brief sketch of each of them follows.

Sarah Frances Fulghum graduated from Bessie Tift College in 1911. After graduation, she taught music and voice at Bessie Tift College. She later graduated from Southern Baptist Theological Seminary in Louisville, Kentucky, became a Baptist missionary to Japan, married a Japanese physician (*Dr. Nobuaki Uehara*, born 3 March 1905, died 2 July 1987), and had two daughters, *Lillian Natsue Uehara* (born 1930) and *Anne Kazue Uehara* (born 1932). Sarah Frances lived in Japan from 1918 until her death in 1973. Her daughters immigrated to the United States after World War II.

Lillian Winefred Fulghum attended Bessie Tift College, Southern Baptist Theological Seminary, and Mercer University. She was a kindergarten teacher in Macon. Never married, she died in Milledgeville State Hospital.

James Hooks Fulghum graduated from Mercer University and attended law school. He married Frances W. Schmidt and they had four children; *Robert Smidtt Fulghum* (born 1929-), *James Hook Fulghum* (born 1933-), *Peter Clapper Fulghum* (born 1934-), and *Frances Matilda Fulghum* (born 1938-).

Charles Bennett Fulghum Sr., MD, married Elizabeth Moore (born 1902- died 1976). They had two sons, *Charles Bennett Fulghum Jr.* (born 1931- died 1995) and *David Dowell Fulghum*, MD (born 1937- died 2011). Charles Bennett Fulghum Sr. graduated from Mercer University and the Medical College of Georgia in Augusta. He practiced medicine at Baldwin Memorial Hospital in Milledgeville, Georgia, until his death in 1976.

Charles Mallary Fulghum (died 3 September 1921). He is buried in Riverside Cemetery, Macon, Georgia.

There is one more Fulghum distant relative: *Robert Lee Fulghum*, who is Lillian and Anne's distant cousin. He is a well-known author who published a book titled *All I Needed to Know I Learned in Kindergarten*.

Sarah Frances, my mother Lillian Winefred
Charles Mallory FulghumMatilda (Slade)
James Hooks Charles Bennett

Mother was raised in a very religious Southern Baptist environment to live and teach the Gospel. I think my mother was eager to leave home, spread her wings, and do something to bring about change in people's hearts, to lead them to Christ.

In those pre-WWI days, young ladies were not permitted to travel alone; they must have a companion if they were to travel out of their environment. What better way to travel and see the world than to be a missionary. Although she never conveyed this idea to us, I really felt my mother wanted to leave Georgia. Georgia was steeped in tradition, do's, don'ts and segregation. To travel would be breaking the invisible chain that bonded her.

When she arrived in Japan in 1918, Mother attended a Japanese language school. Later, she was assigned to be a Maizuru-Yochien's *encho sensei* (Maizuru kindergarten director) for a few years. She also had a certificate to teach kindergarten from the State of Georgia in the USA. When my sister and I were straightening out her belongings after she passed away, we found the certificate stating she was to teach only white children. We were amazed to find such a racially stated certificate of teaching was possible to be handed out to prospective teachers in the South. But that was before 1918, and segregation strongly prevailed.

She was the principal of Maizuru-Yochien in Fukuoka Prefecture, Kyushu, Japan. My mother had a beautiful soprano voice and played the piano well. That is why she opened a glee club for college students who lived in the neighborhood. Some of the students attended different colleges.

Sarah Frances Fulghum with her students at Maizuru-Yochien (kindergarten)

Soon, many students at Seinan-Gakuin College signed up to be in her glee club. They wanted to sing and learn English songs and learn to speak the English language. Mother's evening class became the talk of the college community.

About that time, my father was still in medical school of Kyushu Teikoku Digaku (Imperial University of Fukuoka Prefecture, Kyushu, Japan). He and his friend heard of this young and beautiful American missionary with a golden voice teaching some songs at her home. Father and his friend joined the glee club. I must tell you, Father could not hold a note or carry a tune in an egg basket. Later, when we were growing up and attending Sunday church in Wakayama, I could hear his off-key tone singing. It irritated me so much; one Sunday I asked him to please mouth the words and not try to sing.

Father in back row ——————————— ↓

Mother seated ———↑   English Bible Class and Glee Club, 1922

Although he was tone-deaf and could not carry a tune, Mother graciously accepted my father's enthusiasm. She used to say, "Your father was making joyful noise unto the Lord."

In those days, for a Japanese male even to be thinking about befriending an American female was very unusual, to say the least. In 1973, when my sister and I were cleaning up the house, we found a bunch of letters neatly tied in a faded pink bow. Anne and I read a few letters and realized these were exchanged between our parents as they were falling in love; as we read, we felt like we were invading their privacy.

We knew they were so in love and how difficult it must have been convincing their families to accept a foreigner, overcoming the racial prejudices of each of their families.

Not only the prejudice in color and nationality but they somehow overcome also the differences of their religious belief: Frances being a Christian and a Southern Baptist at that and Nobuaki being a Buddhist.

Nobuaki's uncle Doen was a priest for the Nichiren-Shoshu Buddhism assigned to be the chief priest at Fuji-Daisekiji-Honzan temple in Fukuoka, Japan. He had several hundred followers and was very active in his work. My father stayed at the temple while he was attending college and medical school. Father used to tell me that when he was staying at his uncle's temple, he was awakened every morning by the uncle's chanting while he beat a Taiko drum, "Namiyo Horen Gekkyo," over and over again. Father used to tell me the chanting was as good as an alarm clock. It made such a racket he had no choice but to get up.

During WWII, sake was very difficult to obtain. One parishioner, by mistake, gave Doen methyl alcohol (wood alcohol) instead of grain alcohol to drink. Needless to say, Doen died from methyl alcohol poisoning on the era of Showa 20 (June 23, 1945).

Most young people in Japan, though they are surrounded by Buddhism or Shintoism, are not tied strongly to any religious beliefs. That is why the young medical doctor soon converted to Christianity. My parents were married on June 30, 1928, at their friend Dr. and Mrs. Nemoto's home. Dr. Nemoto was also a prominent physician married to an English lady. No one else attended their wedding, not even their parents. I guess that Dr. and Mrs. Nemoto would be the only ones that understood the true meaning of love and their circumstances of an international mixed-race marriage.

Married on June 30, 1928

When Anne and I were sorting our mother's belongings in the house in Wakayama after she passed away, we found her American passport issued in 1918, when she came to Japan via Vancouver, Canada. She entered Japan through Yokohama and then traveled to Tokyo to enter into a Japanese language school, for one year, before she took her post at Fukuoka, Japan, as a Southern Baptist missionary. Mother spoke fluent Japanese and was able to read and write fairly well. However, I have not seen any Japanese written by her, only her name Ranko Uehara. *Ranko* means "child of the flower orchid." She loved flowers, especially roses, so Mother adopted Ranko as her Japanese name.

After the sorting task was over, Anne and I asked Father what he wanted to do with the love letters they wrote to each other. He wanted us to burn them together with Mother's wedding dress. On the day before we were to return to America, Father helped us dig a pit near the magnolia tree, planted by mother over thirty years ago, and had a little burning ceremony. As we watched the flames consume the letters and the wedding dress, as tears ran down our cheeks while smoke rose up into the sky, we were made to realize how strong our parents' love for each other was throughout these difficult times. What a good example for us to follow.

A True Southern Belle

My image of a Southern belle was established long before I saw the motion picture *Gone with the Wind*. Mother spoke about her childhood, how her mother, Matilda Fulghum, managed her household of domestic help (a cook and several servants). Mother was born May 29, 1890, to a father who was a successful wholesale broker in Macon, Georgia. She used to tell me he often made a fortune one time and went broke at another transaction. It is fairly safe to surmise that money was not a problem in her early years.

No wonder Mother never learned how to cook or did not have any desire to cook. When I was growing up, I never saw a cookbook around the house nor do I remember seeing Mother in the kitchen unless she was giving instructions to the cook.

Mother, being a true Southern belle, most of the time was very sweet and gracious, aware of her station in life—married to a physician who was respected in the community. No wonder, she was a true product of the Southern class system of the era of the eighteen hundreds.

The Japanese class system was strongly established during the Edo period around the year 1600 and the shogunate (the military dictatorship) became the governing body of Japan. Thus, the class system became established. The first and highest class was the samurai or the people in the military position. Although the samurai class was only 10 percent of the total population, they demanded social domination. Then the second class was farmers. The third class, artisans. The fourth class, merchants. The fifth class was the unmentionable underclass group of Buraku people. These people held jobs such as animal slaughtering, and tanning the hides. They often lived by the river and were called the river people.

Mother's family tree can be traced back to the Crusades. She comes from a well-established family in England, and even as I write this story, Mother's relative, an earl named Michal Foljambe, still lives in the eleventh-century Perveril Castle in England. My sister, Anne, met him personally when she made a trip to England. He was surrounded by his ancestral swords and armors from the past. Tideswell, England is the principal seat of the Foljambe family. It is said that the name Fulgham or Fulghum originated from Foljambe. It is believed that repeated poor handwritten official documents throughout the years evolved into the present spelling of Fulghum or Fulgham.

My Japanese Uehara side comes from the Ogasawara Samurai clan on the Kyushu Island of Japan. My great grandfather, Genzo Uehara, served as a samurai attached to the Kokura feudal lord as a kendo teacher and taught other samurai the art of fighting with a Japanese sword.

No doubt it was very easy for Mother to blend into the Japanese class system in 1918 as she arrived in Japan. My birth registration certificate, stating that I was born into a samurai family, was issued by the Fukuoka Prefecture, Yukuhashi township of Japan in 1930. This system of classification was abolished after Meiji restoration, when the Japanese constitution was first written. However, unofficially, classification still remained until after WWII, when the Japanese constitution was rewritten under the direction of General MacArthur.

Mother totally involved herself in Japanese culture. For her daughters, it was not a matter of choice; it was a "must do" from our early age to take classes of flower arrangement and tea ceremony and learn to play the *koto* (Japanese harp). In the year of the Showa seventeenth (1942), a photograph was taken of my mother, a family friend, my sister Kazue, and me seated in front of the famous Nachi Shrine where Mother dedicated her tea ceremony to her beloved Nachi waterfall. The shrine priest gave Mother a *chakin* (a cotton cloth used to wipe the tea cup during tea ceremony) with the Nachi Shrine stamp. I have the cherished *chakin* in my possession.

Mother's flower arrangement

Shinto tea ceremony

Shinto tea cloth

Nachi Water Fall, Wakayama Prefecture

Nachi Falls, Mom Summer of 1942

3 Guests-↓

Anne-↑ Lillian-↑ preparing tea   Father—↑

Lillian's Tea Ceremony

Lillian's flower arrangement

Notes on My Father, Nobuaki Uehara

Note: This is a translation from Japanese of Uehara family history written in 1975 by Dr. Nobuaki Uehara at the request of his daughter, Lillian. It is not a literal translation but is put in English-language story form for ease of reading. Additional comments are by Lillian.

Nobuaki's father, Sakinji, and mother, Toku, lived in Fukuoka Prefecture and had two children.

The firstborn was a girl named Nui (born 1903- died 1924). Nui is remembered as a very smart young lady. She loved to read books written by Natsume Soseki (A famous Japanese writer. Several of his books were translated into English. One book, titled *I'm a Cat*, became famous around the world.)

Nui also loved to read Japanese tanka (short poems) and often composed a few tanka herself. She excelled in shodo (Japanese black ink and brush writing/penmanship). My father remembers her beautiful handwriting.

Nui aspired to become a nurse, and after her graduation from high school, she went to work for her uncle (Toku's younger brother, Dr. Ryutaro Kuwana), who was an otolaryngologist in Tokyo. In 1923, the entire area of Tokyo was destroyed by earthquake and fire. Thousands of people were killed. It also destroyed Dr. Kuwana's clinic and hospital.

Nui escaped the devastating destruction and returned home to Fukuoka Prefecture. Soon after that, she became very ill with tuberculosis and died in December of 1924 while white flakes of snow were softly covering the earth.

Nobuaki remembers that day as though Mother Nature was quietly erasing his sister's short-lived life with the pure white snow. My father told me, "I always regretted my big sister dying at such a young age, just when she was about to discover her own identity and enjoy life."

Nobuaki was the second child of Sakinji and Toku (Kawana) Uehara. He was born on March 3, 1905.

Uehara family Tomb in Yusubaru

Nobuaki died at home, 1-69, Wakaura Higashi, 2-Chome, Wakayama-shi, Japan, July 2, 1987, at 11:10 a.m. His funeral was July 4, 1987. He was cremated and his ashes divided into three parts: 1/3 entombed in the Uehara family plot in Yusubaru, Fukuoka Prefecture, Kyushu Island; 1/3 is entombed at Wakayama Presbyterian Church (church cemetery plot). The address is Nippon Kirisuto Kyodan, Wakayama Kyokai, 7-1 Saikayacho, Wakayama-shi, Japan

Phone (0734) 22-9293, Pastor (as of 1995): Yoshiharu Yamakura

The other 1/3 of the ashes was scattered in Georgia.

Lillian Natsue at Wakayama Church Cemetery, 2003

Nobuaki attended Yukuhashi Primary School, Nakizumi Primary School, and Ichiba Primary School. He attended Ichiba Lower Middle School and graduated from Fukuoka High School. The Japanese school system then comprised: primary school (six years), middle school (four years, two lower, two upper), *Kotogakko* (high school), (two years), and university, (four to five years).

Nobuaki graduated *summa cum laude* (first in his class) as a physician from Japan Imperial University, Department of Medicine, Kyushu. After graduation, he met and married Sarah Frances Fulghum, a Southern Baptist missionary from Macon, Georgia, USA. They were married in the third year of Showa, June 30, 1928, in Fukuoka, at the home of Dr. and Mrs. Nemoto.

Most of the doctors stayed at the university hospital after graduation. Nobuaki, however, because of his marriage, needed additional income, so he went to work at the newly opened Kurume University Medical Section, Department of Dermatology (Kurume Kyushu Igaku Senmon

Gakko), now called Kurume University, Department of Medicine, as an assistant professor. Although he received a higher salary but still in need of more money, he moved to Wakayama City in about one year. He went to work for Dr. Shigeno as the second physician in the doctor's dermatology clinic. With the salary still not being what he wanted, Nobuaki was forced to open his own dermatology clinic in Wakaura, Wakayama City. The clinic, called Immanuel Clinic (Immanuel Iin), was opened in January of the sixth year of Showa (1931).

Clinic sign with Natsue 1931

Dad's clinic and two nurses 1932

Dr. Uehara making house calls

During World War II, Nobuaki was not called for military service although he went on basic training for the infantry medical corps. Because he was married to an American, he surmised he was a possible security risk even though Frances had lost her American citizenship when she married a Japanese national; she had become Japanese. Most physicians from Wakayama were inducted into the military and served overseas.

I remember when we received a phone call from a Japanese military officer stating that although my father's group was in military boot camp and was not allowed visitors, there will be a special consideration on his behalf and that he will be allowed to receive a visitor for two hours.

Since I was the firstborn and though I was about fourteen years old, I could find my way to the military barracks, state my case, and get to visit my father. My mother packed a clean change of clothes and pipe tobacco to take.

I remember it was a very hot day in June or July with humidity as equally high. I walked with a bounce in my gait and soon arrived at the military compound. There were two soldiers standing guard at the gate with fixed bayonets. They looked scary, but I was certain I would be able to convince them to get me through.

I mentioned the officer's name to one of the guards, and he took me to his office. A very neat, fairly young, handsome officer was there.

The officer was seated behind his desk, going through some paperwork. The guard who escorted me to his office knocked on the open door and saluted him and announced my arrival. The officer looked up, smiled, and said, *"Yoku-kimashita ne"* (it was good of you to come) like he was surprised to see such a young girl dressed in high school uniform blouse with "monpe" type of slacks made from my father's old kimono, which I made myself.

Then the officer motioned to the soldier and told him to take me to the dining hall to meet my father. When we crossed the parade ground and entered the large dining hall lined with row upon row of picnic-type tables, I felt like a midget inside a huge cage. Soon, my father walked in with a khaki-colored Japanese military uniform with the same cap as the escorting soldier wore. Dad looked so out of place without his white physician's coat, I could not help but smile. Since I could not run up to him and hug or kiss him like we do at home (that would be improper in public), I could only bow to him and say, "*Otosan ogenki desuka?*"(Father, how are you? Are you well?). Father smiled and said, "*Mane*" (meaning, "so-so").

Father looked thinner and fatigued. No wonder, he had never experienced group living and drills day after day. The meeting only took fifteen minutes. He asked how everyone was doing at home, and I gave him the exchange of clothes that I brought. In return, he gave me the soiled underwear for me to take home. Then the same soldier came to escort me back to the front gate. I felt very privileged to get to see my father, even for a short time. No other physician was that lucky.

Later, my nurse said to me that that officer was once a patient of my father, and he wanted to reciprocate my father's kindness of healing him.

After 1945, Nobuaki was elected president of the Wakayama Doctor's Association. He was well liked and helped to establish the association's banking system with Sumitomo Bank. He served three terms, a total of nine years. He was then elected to presidency of the Prefecture (State) Medical Association and was taken away from his practice so much.

Nobuaki was a very sincere Christian and worked very hard to practice what he felt was right for the good of everyone. He served as an elder in the Wakayama Presbyterian Church for many years.

Immediately post World War II, the American Army's Fifty-fourth Evacuation Hospital was established in Wakayama City to repatriate American POWs through Wakayama Harbor (the only harbor that was not a mine field and that was large enough to allow the anchoring of a hospital ship). Nobuaki's fluency in English facilitated the speedy translation of Japanese medical records on POWs, and he became a liaison to the American physicians of the Fifty-fourth Evacuation Hospital staff.

He was an avid reader and spoke three languages fluently: Japanese, English, German, and some French. When he was in his thirties, he studied Esperanto, which was supposed to become the universal language. He became a pen pal with another student of the language and exchanged many letters and cards over the years. My father kept many of these letters and postcards.

He had many avocations. His main interest was in photography and made his own cameras by building a box that was capable of interchanging lenses. He developed his own film in a darkroom he had converted from a closet in his clinic. His daughters always had to pose for him when they were in their teens.

Nobuaki suffered multiple strokes (CVA) before his death, but each time, he would recover. He was ordered by his physician friend to take long walks to help in the recovery process. During this time, he developed an interest in photographing and documenting the stone dog statue that stood in front of Japanese temples and shrines. He became so engrossed in this hobby that he published a book about the history of Komainu (temple dogs). Sumitomo Bank of Wakayama asked to display his photographs in one of their exhibits. It generated much interest in the community. He used to tell his daughters, "The dogs are not fickle like humans. They are always waiting for me faithfully in front of the temples."

One temple dog picture he took

Nobuaki's interest in medicine led him to do private experiments on rabbits and guinea pigs. There were rabbit hutches lined up in the courtyard between his clinic and his home, and his wife was always afraid that their children would catch some skin disease from the experimental animals. As a result of his experiments, Nobuaki was able to successfully treat psoriasis, and his daughters remember people coming from far away cities to receive his medications. When his daughters urged him to publish his work, his only comment was that it needed more research before he could be assured of its success. He died before completion of the research, and his notes were given to a relative, Hideichi Abe, a dermatologist practicing medicine in Hiroshima, Japan. Hideichi is the son of Sakinji's sister, Sakae's daughter, Mitsuno.

Nobuaki insisted he would keep his clinic open until his death, and he kept his promise to himself. Although he was urged by his daughters to retire and take it easy, he saw patients up to the last day before he died.

Nobuaki is remembered by his two daughters, Lillian Natsue and Anne Kazue, as a very brilliant man, who never boasted about his achievements. He was filled with compassion for humanity and, most of all, very loyal to his wife, his family, and friends. He would give people the very shirt off his back if they were to ask for it. He served as an inspiration to his daughters to do their best in their walk through life.

Home Sweet Home

I remember every winter night my younger sister, Anne Kazue, and I would sit together in an oversized oak chair with large oak arms, which had a very comfortable futon as a cushion. We must have been not more than five and three years old because I remember the chair was so comfortable even with two of us with our knees drawn up almost to our chins so our skirts can cover our feet to keep them warm. Remember, I grew up in Japan in the 1930s, and Japanese homes did not have automatic central heating system as you do. So at times, it was very cold even inside in the house. We would huddle up to an iron two-coil electric stove that had a kettle of hot water steaming to keep the room vaporized and to make ready for tea.

Mother would select a fairy tale from her collection of English books—*Uncle Remus*, *Br'er Rabbit* (Brother Rabbit), or *Aesop's Fables*—and would read to us in English. When she read for half an hour, we would always have an intermission, and Mother would peel us a huge, very shiny red apple or an apple called golden delicious, which was greenish yellow in color. It was so large that one apple was enough for both of us.

As she was reading, my eyes would wander through the room, which was about fifteen by seventeen feet and had a *tokonoma* (an alcove of honor). Mother always had a beautiful flower arrangement and some kind of a scroll of Japanese calligraphy or a painting—whatever was appropriate for the four seasons or the occasion, such as girls' festival in March or boys' festival in May. We were always taught to admire the flower arrangement and appreciate the beauty of its shape, asymmetry, and color. The *tokonoma* also had a very narrow, tall mahogany bookcase with suede leather-bound, gold-edged parchment paper pages. There were twenty-nine volumes of the eleventh edition encyclopedia (1910-1911), which was my mother's pride and joy. She told us it belonged to a very good missionary friend who retired and went back to the United States. We were permitted to look through the very large beautiful pages to look at the illustrations. I guess that was one of Mother's ways to encourage us to read.

Then my eyes would take me to the opposite side of the room which had our mother's Yamaha baby grand piano, which our father purchased for my mother not too long after we moved into this house. A typhoon destroyed our previous home just across the street. As we played around the house, we could always hear our mother at her beloved piano playing some classical music, an operetta, or her favorite hymns. People passing by our home would later comment how nice it sounded.

Yamaha Baby Grand Piano, Anne, Lillian, and Mother

Next, my eyes would lock onto a very delicately constructed French provincial sofa and two high-backed chairs flanking the sofa. They were covered with plush blue velvet with a fleur-de-lis pattern. The round pedestal table made in the same fashion had a beautiful cut-glass top, which completed the ensemble. Everything was in its place and looked very elegant.

The oversized oak chair was placed next to a very large RCA Victor Victrola, which was operated by a hand crank. The cabinet had knobby legs with eagle claws, which stood on the highly polished wooden floor. Mother would dust the large twelve-inch-diameter one-sided record with a hole in the middle after she carefully lifted it out from its case.

Very carefully, she would place the large record on the turntable matching the post on the turntable with the hole in the middle of the record and lowered it until the record came to rest on the felt-covered turntable; then the arm of a very sharp needle was lowered to the record. The magnificent tenor voice of opera singer Caruso would boom out of the Victrola. At times, we were allowed to place a record that had the well-known song "Old Man River." We were fascinated with the turntable turning the record round and round but more so with the two little old-fashioned Mickey and Minnie Mouse holding their hands as they danced across the large record. Mother said their felt shoes kept the records clean so as to prevent the needle from picking up lint.

I hope this explanation helps you visualize what I had to do in order to listen to one piece of music when all you have to do now is to place a four-and-a-half-inch plastic disc into a disc player or download music to your iPod and listen for hours to your favorite songs.

Facing the *tokonoma* (the alcove of honor) to the right and to its left were verandas, which had sliding glass doors the length of the room. They were like *shoji* screens, but instead of paper, the doors had glass panels to let in the sunlight. Since the room had no windows, these large glass doors were the only means to get fresh air and sunlight into the room. Mother always had some delicate lace curtains on these glass doors to enhance the ambiance.The other side of the veranda also had a set of those glass panels to protect the wooden veranda from the rain. The glass doors were protected by another set of sliding storm shutters, which were called *amado*.

After an hour of reading, mother would slowly close the book and take her clip-on spectacles off her nose and say, "That's all for tonight," then would kiss both of us on the forehead. I remember my mother's melodious Southern accent while the tea kettle quietly vaporized the living room and her warm lips ever so softly touching our foreheads, then saying good night.

Kewpie Doll

I was told that Mother was hospitalized at the Wakayama Red Cross Hospital in labor, having my sister Kazue Anne. I was left under the care of my nanny playing with my big Kewpie doll. I was two years old and the oversized celluloid doll was almost as large as I was.

When I was growing up, plastics were not invented yet; toys were made from either wood, iron, tin, lead, or celluloid. When I look back, none of our toys would meet the present manufacturing safety standards for toys and, at times, were even harmful to babies' health. It's a wonder we even lived after playing with those toys painted with lead-based paint.

At any rate, I was on the upstairs balcony, looking down at the front garden with the Kewpie doll in my arms, having a good time. Those days, my father's medical clinic occupied the downstairs, and the living quarters were over the clinic. Fortunately, my father was in his clinic treating patients and just happened to step into his pharmacy to mix some powdered medication for his patient. The window was open, and he saw me sail by the window with the oversized doll in my arms. The very frightened nanny was screaming her head off, calling my name from the upstairs balcony. Fortunately, the Kewpie doll foiled my fall and I was alive without a scratch, but with the wind knocked out of my lungs. I was not hurt but would not cry or talk. The usually talkative "chatty Kathy" was silent. So the story goes.

My father rushed me to the Red Cross Hospital's emergency room, and my mother came down from her hospital room to see me. Just when she picked me up in her arms, I started crying and said Ma Ma, and all was well. My family used to tease me when I acted stupid or said crazy things that the fall was the cause of my craziness.

Temple-Chan

My growing-up years in Japan were very happy years. I knew I was different from the typical Japanese children with straight shiny pitch-black hair bobbed like a Japanese doll. My hair was light brown and curly; no matter how I struggled to straighten it by wetting my hair, it would just curl up. Ringlets covered my head. Mother would brush it several times a day and tell me how pretty I looked. But like any other child anywhere in the world, I wanted to look like the other children around me.

When I was about five years old, this feeling soon faded when Shirley Temple came onto the scene. Instantly, I became famous around my hometown. Soon, I was called Temple-Chan because my hair resembled hers and my round face and cheeks shined under the ringlets of brown hair. You see, all movies shown in my childhood were not made in color; they were all in black-and-white film, so no one knew Shirley Temple had blond hair. That is pretty funny, don't you think?

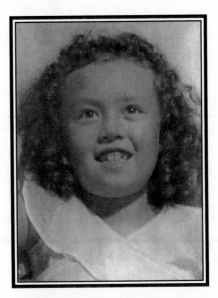

Lillian, seven years, Temple-Chan

Once, after I grew up and in my late forties, I went back to see my parents in my hometown. I was in the large crosswalk in front of the Wakayama Castle with my sister, Anne, deep in conversation, when a gentle touch from the back and the word *Temple-Chan* came across my right shoulder. Startled, I looked back only to see a Catholic nun smiling at us, saying, "I don't know you in person, but I heard about you often from your mother." My mother and the sister met when both of them attended an interdenominational conference in Osaka, Japan. I thought that was pretty unique: a Catholic nun and my mother, a Protestant missionary, connected together because of Shirley Temple. My mother is gone now, but I still correspond with the nun now in her late eighties in Wakayama City at Christmastime.

My Beautiful Green Dress

When I was about five years old, my parents decided to take a vacation for one week, to stay at a seaside resort away from our town, to get away from the demanding work schedule of my father.

Until then, my sister and I had never been on a vacation with both of our parents. They waited until their children were of the right age to travel. Of course, we took day trips to parks or special playgrounds on Sunday afternoon after we attended church and had a nice lunch at a restaurant.

My mother purchased new dresses for both of us to wear. My dress, with a large Peter Pan collar, was a pale green color, the color of young bamboo. It was decorated with white lace around the edge. Several embroidered pink rosebuds were on the bodice of the dress. The bodice was attached to a gathered skirt and a big bow to be tied at the back.

When Mother came home to show us the dresses she had purchased for us, I instantly fell in love with my dress. I pictured how I would look in my dress, walking like a princess with both parents at my side. "Surely, I will be the talk of the town."

The reservation for the resort in Shirahama was confirmed. Shirahama, a resort town south of our city, was famous for its pure white sand beaches, aquarium, and whaling ships. The town had a museum about whales and whaling ships. I could hardly wait. The day finally arrived; our bags were packed, and we were ready for our long-awaited vacation.

The time came to put on my beautiful green dress. I was able to dress myself by that age while my mother was busy dressing my sister. All she had to supervise was that I wore the correct socks and put on my patent leather shoes. I put on my cotton underwear, my petticoat, and finally the green dress that I adored. I felt my collar was scratching my neck. Thinking it was the dress label tickling me, I asked my mother to straighten it out. She came to look at my collar and told me there were several blisterlike bumps on my neck. Having been a kindergarten teacher, she immediately knew I had chicken pox. She calmly told me to take off the dress so she could examine me. Not knowing anything about chicken pox, I was horrified to think some bug would bite me all over my body. My father came and confirmed that I had chicken pox. "So what, I had chickenpox. I can still go with you!" The answer was devastating to a five-year-old child who is looking for a fun-filled vacation!

Mother decided to stay home with me and urged Father to take my sister and two of our nurses in our place since Father's clinic was already closed for the few days. They all left a little later than the planned departure time, promising me they would bring back a special *omiyage* (a gift).

My beautiful green dress was hung on a hanger where I could see it at the foot of my bed. I began to spike a fever, and Mother took good care of me. That night I dreamed about playing in the sand at the seashore with all the rest of my family; I was having fun.

When I awoke the next morning, it was comforting to know Mother and my beautiful green dress were still at my side.

Fun Play under the Sun and Stars

My sister and I were very fortunate to have a mother who was trained in child development. She was very aware in teaching us how to enjoy constructive play. Not only did she read to us a lot but also paid attention to our creative play. In the summer months during week days, Mother would pack a picnic basket and take us to Kataonami beach close to our home. This beach was unique: it had a long white sand beach that was lined with pine trees over a hundred years old with their large roots exposed. Many years of strong winds blowing on the pine roots dug away the sand and exposed the roots. Now it was an ideal place to play house.

Each of us would pick a suitable tree with large roomy roots to establish a living room, kitchen, and a dining room. We took our tea sets and other play toys to set up a *mama-goto* (playhouse). Mother would be our house guest and come to visit each home. We would pretend to serve tea and cookies made from seaweed and sand or sand dollars found on the beach.

We played all afternoon, and when evening came, at times our father would take time out from his clinic and join us in swimming. Both of my parents were good swimmers. My father was on the long-distance swim team in college and received a medal. My parents must have enjoyed their little free time swimming together in the warm summer ocean.

The ocean was warm and clear. The small waves would lap at our feet occasionally, and when the tide and the season were just right, glistening plankton would cover our bodies. When we emerged from the water in the evening near dusk, our bathing suits would shimmer and glisten like a dress on a princess. My sister and I would pretend we were Tinker Bell or some princess going to a ball all dressed in silver slippers shimmering in the moonlight. When the plankton stopped glistening, we would get back in the water only to emerge as a different imaginary princess.

Since my birthday was in August, I remember my parents would give me a beach party at the swimming facility. My best recollection was that, in place of a birthday cake, I asked for a watermelon all to myself. I would eat to my heart's content and my stomach so full that it bulged out. To this day, I'm very fond of watermelon.

Lillian's fourth birthday party at the beach restaurant

Our parents would watch us and equally enjoy their children having a good time. Little did we realize then that WWII was looming in the future and it would shatter our happy dreams.

Grandfather Sakinji and Grandmother Toku

Sakinji Uehara was born to a proud samurai family. My great-grandfather, Genzo Uehara, was a Japanese swordsmanship instructor for the Ogasawara Clan, which had its castle in the north side of Kyushu Island, Kokura. Swordsmanship instructors ranked pretty high among the ranks of samurai.

Kokura Castle   Photo by author, 1989

The Meiji restoration in 1868 abolished all class system in Japan. Thus, some Samuri Clan revolted against the Meiji "equality system." The Ogasawara Clan fought against the Choshu Clan and lost the skirmish. The beautiful Kokura Castle was reduced to ashes. Thus, the Ogasawara Clan was resolved, and all the samurai were scattered throughout Kyushu Island. This is how my great-grandfather, stripped of his proud rank, came to Yusubaru Village with his family where my grandfather was born. Sakinji grew up to be a skilled electrician working in the coal mines of Kyushu Island. Grandfather had many hobbies; one was to carve wood and make toys for children. I have a photograph showing a pony-sized horse, which my grandfather carved for his son. My father is on it looking proud as punch, with Nui, his older sister, by his side. He looked to be between the ages of three and five years old.

Horse carved by Sakinji Uehara

My grandfather served in the Russian Japanese War (1904, the thirty-seventh year of Emperor Meiji) and received a medal. My grandmother Toku was known to have high intelligence. She had osteoporosis and walked with her back almost bent over.

Toku was able to discuss politics and any other world events. She could do only limited housework due to her physical condition. Thus, she read constantly to pass the time. My grandfather helped her by doing more of the housework, which was very unusual for a Japanese man to do so much woman's work in those days.

The kitchen was attached to one of the front rooms, and one had to change shoes to step down onto the dirt floor. There was a sink and a well that one had to pump by hand to bring up the water to wash dishes. That was the only source of water for the entire house. We were used to having running tap water, so when we saw the pump, we were intrigued and wanted to help Grandfather pump the water from the well.

The kitchen also had one large *kamado* (wood-burning fireplace) on which a large rice cooker fitted. The other fire pit could be used for cooking or broiling food. It was a very primitive but adequate arrangement.

Drawing as I remember Sakinji and Toku's house

When my sister and I were kindergarten age, we all took a trip to Kyushu to see our grandparents. It was spring vacation time and the cherry blossoms were in full bloom. The country house was quite small—only two large rooms with an attached veranda, built against a hill next to a large pond. The pond was used by the farmers to irrigate their vegetable garden. Grandfather took us up the hill and showed us the pond full of tadpoles. We saw not just one or two, but they were packed around the pond with their long-tailed black bodies as big as teaspoons. My sister and I scooped some up into our small buckets and carried them down to the house to watch them grow.

That evening, both my sister and I helped Grandfather pump the water for our baths into the *ofuro* (a round cedar hot tub). The hot tub was outside in the back garden underneath a cherry tree and was heated by a wood-burning boiler. My sister and I were happy to take a bath in such a unique bathtub. Mother helped us soap up and wash our hair first by pouring warm water from the tub over our heads outside the tub. Then we stood in the tub together with our heads above the water to splash and soak. Looking back, it was a very picturesque scene soaking under the flowering cherry tree with petals gently floating down. It was quite an exciting day, and I doubt we had any problems going to sleep.

The next day, we entertained our grandparents by creating a skit. We sang kindergarten songs and danced around the room. I remember opening and closing the *fusuma* (a solid paper sliding door), which separated the two rooms. We pretended it was the stage curtain. Every time we opened the *fusuma*, everyone clapped in anticipation of the next skit.

When time came for us to leave for home, my sister remembered the tadpoles and wanted to take them with us. My grandfather tried convincing my sister to return the poor tadpoles to their home. After all, they were separated from their mother for almost three days, and they were crying to see their mother. My sister finally agreed that the tadpoles should go home to the lake, and she took them back. Though this trip was almost seventy-five years ago, those happy memories linger on.

Lillian, Grandmother Toku, Anne, and Sakinji Uehara

Preschool Years — Kindergarten

I must have enjoyed my kindergarten years so much so that I remember many happy hours with my teachers and my friends. Wakayama Yochien (Wakayama Kindergarten), on a hillside facing the famous Wakayama Castle, was built near the primary school, which I attended later.

Every day, I had to catch the street car at Wakaura-Guchi electric tram stop near my home and ride past seven stations until I came to the stop near the kindergarten. I always had fun on the streetcar talking to my girlfriends or, when the conductor was not looking, swinging on the leather straps before other adult passengers came on the tram. There were five of us catching the tram every morning from where we lived, and the conductor knew each of us by name. If one of us did not happen to show up, he would ask if so-and-so was ill or just late.

My class was called Momo Gumi, which meant peach blossom group. There were Sakura Gumi, which meant cherry blossom group, and Ume Gumi, which meant plum blossom group. With each change of season, the teacher would put up colorful cutouts or pictures appropriate to the occasion. When parent-teacher day came, my mother's hat and Western clothing would always give her position away among the kimono-clad black-haired Japanese mothers standing at the back of the class room, observing class activities.

Kindergarten class   ↑—Top Row, Lillian Natsue Uehara

She is seventh from the left side.

Autumn, with cloudless blue skies and gentle cool breeze, was a welcome change from the hot and sticky summer we experienced just a few weeks prior. Everyone was ready for having a big *undokai* (field day). The relay running, short-distance running, and all types of group and individual events all made us hungry for the ever-so-good *bento* (lunch boxes) packed with rice balls, some teriyaki chicken, cucumber salad and pickles, and tea. *Undokai* was usually held on a national holiday or on a Sunday, so both parents were present and could participate in the fun: parent-and-child games like the three-legged running race or the ever-popular egg-in-a-spoon race, etc. My sister was a fast runner and always came in first.

One could count on my sister winning the race. So when it came time for choosing partners for a relay, she was always chosen first. I could not run fast, even when my life depended on it, and always came in last. My family would tease me and say, "Here comes lead bottom *Onatsu* (my nickname) holding up the rear." To this day, I cannot run fast.

Kindergarten field play and rice pounding

Kindergarten excursion   ↑——————— Lillian in front of teacher

Picking choke cherries

Never a Dull Moment

Tamaki Miura (born 1884-died 1946) was a renowned Japanese opera singer. After her graduation from Tokyo Music Conservatory in 1914, she went abroad to Berlin, Germany, for her studies as an opera singer. Ms. Miura first came to the United States to perform the famous *Madam Butterfly* in 1917.

It is not clear when Mother, a soprano singer and a music teacher, met Ms. Miura and cultivated their friendship.

When I was about six years old, one day, my mother told me not to attend school and to put on my Sunday best clothes, and then she took me to Osaka City on the interurban train. When we arrived at the large concert hall in Osaka, I still did not know what I was about to encounter. Mother took me backstage to see Ms. Miura. The opera star greeted Mother like a long-lost friend and looked at me with loving eyes. She told my mother that when the performance ended and the time came for an encore, she would like for me to come onto the stage with her to dedicate a song to her old friend, Mrs. Sarah Frances Uehara. Mother was surprised but very pleased that this world-renowned opera star would think to honor her in such a fashion.

This was the first time I sat through an opera that lasted almost two hours with an intermission between curtain breaks.

The time came for the encore. Ms. Miura motioned for me to come up onto the stage. We were seated very close to the stage, so it did not take long for me to walk up the steps to the stage and next to Ms. Miura. I remember she was dressed in a Japanese kimono with a large *uchikake*, an oversized padded kimono loosely hung over her shoulder with the hem trailing on the ground.

Ms. Miura motioned for me to come closer to her and announced to the audience that this song will be dedicated to her friend and the mother of her daughter, Natsue, standing next to her.

To a small child, Ms. Miura looked so tall and bulky with all the layers of kimono. She placed her hand on my shoulder and started to sing. While she was singing, she moved back and forth, side to side, pulling me around with her. Soon, her hand slipped from my shoulder to around my neck and ear. I felt like I was being dragged across the stage with each movement. Yet I was mindful not to step on the trailing hem of her kimono.

To a small child, it was not fun, but I kept looking up at Ms. Miura with a smile on my face as my mother told me to do. The song she sang seemed to last a long time. I know encores do not last but a few minutes, but as a child, it lasted way too long. Finally, when she stopped singing, my neck and ears were red from the friction of her hand and the heavily embroidered kimono sleeve rubbing on the side of my face and neck as she moved around the stage. Ms. Miura told me to bow with her, and together we exited the stage, leaving the sound of ovations and bravas behind us.

Next to the experience of getting my tonsils out with only a local anesthesia, this painful experience with the opera singer will never be forgotten.

Miura, Tamaki

↑————Lillian, presenting flowers

Fuzoku-Shogakko, Primary School

The primary school I attended was attached to the Wakayama prefecture Shihan Gakko (Normal School). The school took pride in high academic standing. It was said that if one graduated from this school, it was almost assured that one would be able to enter prefectural high school.

Fuzoku (meaning "attached to something") required an entrance physical exam and oral exam of applicants and only took the so-called brightest children. I will never forget the day of the oral examination.

Mother dressed me in a Sunday-going-to-church dress and combed my hair in long ringlets hanging around my face with a big bow in my hair. I thought I looked pretty cute myself. We rode the streetcar and got off in front of the school. I was quite familiar with this station stop since until a few weeks ago, I traveled this way to my kindergarten getting off at this station.

A winding road up the steep hill, lined with large pine trees, took us up to the iron gates of the school flanked by concrete pillars. Just inside was a bronze statue of a boy dressed in tattered clothes, carrying cut logs on his back, reading a book. I told my mom that his name was Ninomiya Kinjiro. I told her that I learned about him in kindergarten and how his family was so poor he had to work by gathering kindling in the woods for sale to support his family. However, he wanted to learn so badly that he took every moment of his spare time to read. That was his pleasure and desire to learn. Later, he became a very learned and famous man.

As we walked up the walkway, we came to the large building entrance with tables to register. We found my name easily according to the Japanese alphabet. *Uehara*, in the English alphabet, is almost at the end, but in the Japanese alphabet, it is the third vowel (*A, I, U, E, O*).

Mother signed me in. The large room with a stage was to be the waiting room for the applicants and their parents. We sat quietly without saying anything. Soon, several children's names were called, and they were to follow one teacher to a room with a large table with four people sitting behind it. There must have been several exam rooms like this one to accommodate the large number of children taking the examination.

When it was my turn, I entered the room, bowed, and stood at attention until I was told to sit in the chair in front of the table. Looking back, I remember the teachers—two men and two women—were smiling and they took turns asking questions. First, my name, then what my father did, how many siblings, and so on. I guess that was to put me at ease. I answered all the questions without hesitation. The big question was coming next. A teacher asked me, "Do you know the story of Momotaro?"

Momotaro (Peach Boy) stories are told in Japan as a bedtime story to every child, so I knew it well.

The teacher said, "Let's hear about it from the beginning." I said, "Hai," and started with "*Mukashi mukai sonomukai* (meaning 'long, long time ago'), there lived an old man and an old woman. They sadly had no children, etc."

I told you the story, Justin, Brittany and Briana, as you grew up. So you know all about Peach Boy. I have an English translation of the Peach Boy with pictures and all so you can teach your children about the Peach Boy story.

Anyway, half way through the story, one teacher said, "That is good, thank you. You don't have to go on." I said, "But that's only half the story. There is more." I was pretty upset that they did not want to hear the story anymore. The good part was yet to come and also the song called "Momotaro San" that came with the story. I knew it all and wanted to sing that song from beginning to end. One of the teachers said, "We know you know it so well that we do not have to ask you to tell us more." That must have satisfied me; I stopped talking.

I learned later that the exams were testing the children for how sociable they are and their ability to memorize and retain what they had learned.

The school I was about to enter needed fairly bright, well-adjusted children for the normal school students to teach the practicum.

The physical exam must have been done prior to the oral exam, but I don't remember anything about it.

When I came out of the room and was led back to the room with waiting parents, my mother asked me, "How did it go?" I said without hesitation, "Very good," and started telling her how much fun it was to tell the teachers the story of Momotaro and how put out I felt when they told me to stop. Until this day, it remains in my memory so very vividly. The experience must have made a big impression on me.

I had to take many oral exams later in my life as I wrote my thesis in graduate school and had to defend what I wrote, as well as each time my career changed and interviews were given. I never was once afraid or nervous about taking oral exams. I guess my very first experience put me at ease. Since then, it has been smooth sailing.

Classes Begin

After passing the entrance exam with flying colors, I started school with the entrance ceremony in March 1936. The girls were dressed in sailor suit tops with pleated skirts, all looking so clean and crisp. The boys were in the usual navy blue mandarin collar uniform with brass buttons going down the front of their jackets.

First grade uniform with book bag

The first day of school started with each teacher calling out each student's name, all twenty-five of them, and introducing himself. He told us to follow him to the classroom. There were two classrooms to a grade. They were named A Gumi (group A) and B Gumi (group B); I was in B Gumi. Attached to each class were three to four young students in their twenties learning to be teachers themselves in the stages of student-teaching practicum.

When I look back, I think we were very fortunate to have so many able-bodied teachers helping us to get ahead.

First grade B-Gumi (Class)   ↑— Lillian, top row

If one of us did not understand some problem in math class, we held our hand up and there was a student teacher at our side assisting us with the problem. Therefore, all the students in our class were able to progress at the same pace, no one lagged behind. What an ideal situation for both teachers and students. Most of the student teachers were men. I did not encounter any women teachers during the whole six years of grade school. Only the home economics teacher, who taught sewing, was a woman in her forties, very kind but strict.

It was there, in my third grade, that I learned to sew straight stitches, cross-stitches, and *kuke nui*, which is a type of cross-stitch used to hem skirts and kimonos so they will not unravel so quickly. We first made one double-layered cleaning cloth called *zokin*. Every Japanese family used them. It was simple to make, and we were able to use all the different stitches we had learned. Next, we made a simple apron with a pocket gathered at the waist.

By the time we were in sixth grade, we were able to make our own cotton Japanese kimono worn in the summer called a *yukata*.

My stitches used to be too short or too long, sometimes wavy and very uneven. The teacher would make me take the stitches out and sew it over. I don't remember how many times I had to redo my *Zokin*, but finally I got it straight. Now I can hand sew most anything very neatly and straightly. Thanks to good training I had.

Fuzoku, my school, was attached to the Normal School—separated by a fence and a playground—coupled with a basketball court, tennis court, and a very large swimming pool, very deep at one end with a large diving board. This is where I really learned to swim.

One day in July, all our classmates were taken to the Normal School swimming pool to be taught how to swim. I must have been in second or third grade. The instructors told us to practice holding our breath underwater. Then the next day, several swimming styles were taught as we held on to the side of the pool. The teachers were right beside us showing us how to use our hands and legs like a frog. This was fun, but no matter how hard I tried to swim, I could not advance. This went on for about three days, and I was very frustrated and discouraged that some classmates were swimming by now, not in the best form maybe but at least making headway. That evening, I went to bed praying that God would help me, somehow, so I will be able to swim by the end of the week. During that night, I dreamt that I could swim just like a frog using my hands and legs in synchronization. The next day, everyone watching me was amazed that I could swim; it felt so good. I was so happy, only to be awakened by my sister saying that I was kicking her in bed.

What a disappointment it was to find out that it was only a dream. However, I decided if I can swim so well in my dreams, I can do it for real. The next morning, when I went back to school for the swimming class, much to my amazement, I was able to relax, tread water, and swim just like in my dreams. This time for real I was making headway.

Hitler's Youth Came to Kobe, Japan

Adolf Hitler became chancellor of Germany on January 30, 1933. I was only three years old. I must have been no more than nine or ten years old at the time when German influence became very strong in Japan. One day, the Hitler's youth group came to Kobe, Japan, for a goodwill tour. For some reason, my parents received an invitation to attend a reception in their honor.

Kobe is about one hundred kilometers from Wakayama, and we had to take an electric train first to Osaka and then transfer to another train to Kobe. Kobe is a port town with a large harbor and docks, bustling with incoming and outgoing ships from all over the world. The town itself was built up on the hillside dotted with red brick buildings of mansions, churches, and shops. This town housed many foreigners (gaijin) from around the world and had special shops selling unusual and unique items. The harbor can be viewed from the hillside, glistening in the sun or, at times, being shrouded with fog. I used to love to go to Kobe tagging after Mother shopping for chocolates and to see foreign towheaded blue-eyed children.

I was not told from whom or why my parents received the invitation to Hitler's youth reception, but as a child, I was delighted to have a chance to see some foreigners and get to eat some delicious sweets. My sister and I were dressed in our Sunday best, and Mother had her best dress with a wide-brimmed picturesque hat with white gloves.

It was midmorning when we arrived at the reception. Stepping out of the taxi, we were greeted royally by some person speaking German to my parents. My father spoke fluent German because of his medical background, and my mother, because of her musical background. My sister and I did not understand a word the usher had said, but we silently followed our parents through beautifully manicured lawn bordered with red and yellow flowers. Finally, we came into a clearing lined with rows and rows of white lawn chairs. There were several large tables draped with white linen tablecloths. Each table had a large vase of flowers. Between the decorations were many large platters laden with finger sandwiches, cakes, cookies, even chocolates, nuts, and mints. Our mouths were watering because it was almost noon, and we had traveled all morning to get there. Anne and I were all eyes because there were so many *gaijins* gathered.

The speech started soon after our arrival with about twenty towheaded Hitler's youth in there khaki uniforms standing in a row between German and Japanese flags. With fresh clean-cut hair and clean faces glistening in the early summer sun, I thought they looked very impressive, but my eyes were still drawn to the food table close to us. More than likely having children with them, our parents asked to be seated near the back to have close access to the WC. My sister and I were taught to lift one or two fingers whenever we needed to use the water closet instead of blurting out loud that we needed to excuse ourselves.

Midway into the speech, I noticed that my parents were whispering something softly to each other, nodding their heads. Very suddenly, they stood up, took our hands, and started to walk out of the garden and into the awaiting taxi outside the gate. All the time, we were protesting that we had not eaten yet and that we were hungry. Even as a child, I sensed that something was not right for my parents to look that seriously upset and to leave a gathering place like they were on fire.

When we reached Osaka, we were treated to a very special American meal at one of our favorite Fujiya restaurants. Later, when it was safe to discuss, we were told that my parents had a different philosophy than the people at the gathering and that they did not wish to associate with them. Only after WWII was over I understood why my parents left that gathering in such a hurry.

Middle and High School Years

In Japan, the new school year always started in April and ended in March. Well into the spring of 1943, school has just started. We were told that the principal had something to tell us all. The girls were assembled outside in the parade ground, waiting impatiently to hear what the *kocho sensei* (principal) had to say. I remember so well because the warm spring sun felt good on our faces and the balmy sea breeze gently brushed over our cheeks. I was thirteen years old and WWII had just started. Although I knew my country was at war, things seemed the same around our hometown. Nothing had changed except for some hustle and bustle around the Japanese military base and barracks. More young men were enlisting or receiving induction notices.

Finally, after standing around for fifteen minutes, our principal arrived and climbed the podium, looking very serious. After a few seconds, he announced that, henceforth, there will be half-day sessions in the morning, and after our lunch break, we will separate into three to five student groups to go into the field to help the farmers with whatever tasks they assigned us to do.

My friends were all shocked to learn that, regardless of our skill levels, we were all going to be inducted into the *Gakuto doin*. (This means inducting the students to work in factories or any other place the government needed them for manpower.) With manpower diminishing and with the war effort getting stronger, we had all heard rumors that all younger school children might be organized to work in the fields with the farmers and their family, and older children, fourteen and up, will be sent to work in the factories to augment the lack of manual labor needed to run the machinery in the factories.

Lillian, Anne in middle school uniform

We were young children, not knowing how serious the war situation had become. We all rejoiced that we had to attend school for only half a day, and then we got to go outdoors to "work in the fields." To us, this was just like play, or so we thought.

Little did we realize then that we were going to be deprived of an important portion of middle school education. To this day, I believe we were cheated out of important fundamental knowledge that was so crucial to obtain prior to our adult years.

That day, when we returned home to report what was going to happen the next day, my parents were not surprised and just told me to be careful. The next day after our lunchtime, many farmers came to school to pick us up. I was assigned, with two other girls, to a farmer that had a large *daikon* (white long radish) and other vegetable gardens. The two other girls were farmers' daughters and were experienced with tending crops. I had never even touched dirt except to plant morning glory seeds in a clay pot for a school science project. You know, one of those assignment projects to plant the seed and watch it grow.

The two girls were immediately assigned to the field to cut weeds out of the rows and rows of vegetables. The farmer looked at me and decided to hand me over to his wife. She gave me the job of babysitting so she could go to work in the field helping her husband.

I was delighted that she felt safe to trust me with her baby boy. I had no idea about changing diapers or feeding the infant. She quickly told me what to do—to change diapers. The diapers were made out of old cotton kimonos. She strapped the six-month-old baby on my back, and off she went to the field telling me to follow her to the grassy knoll.

It was a nice spring day, and as we were walking up and down the narrow rice paddy paths, the infant promptly went to sleep. Plastic-lined pants for babies had not been invented yet, so all I had between the infant and my back was a thin layer of a rubberized small sheet of cloth, which apparently slipped askew. After walking for an hour, I felt a warm wet feeling on my back, which told me something was not right. Yes, the baby and the wet diaper were stuck to my back. That was the clue to change his diaper. When I got back home that night, my parents laughed and told me I was now an experienced babysitter.

The next day, we knew where to go and went directly to the same farm. We were fed lunch that consisted of rice gruel with sweet potatoes mixed in, a sour pickled plum, and some cooked vegetable, *daikon* from the garden. It tasted very good. Japan depended on merchant marine shipments of commodities into the country. The ships were torpedoed and sank before they could reach their destination. Exotic foods like candies and chocolate were difficult to obtain. We still had plenty of fish, seaweed, chicken, eggs, and some beef available at the marketplace.

June and July were called *Tsuyu* (the rainy season). All the farmers were so busy planting rice. This was the season all hands were needed, even the inexperienced hands like ours. Knee-deep in the rice paddy, we were taught to plant *nae* (small starter rice plants looking almost like weeds). One must push the plant about two inches down into the gluelike mud with three fingers and pack the mud around it with the rest of the fingers to prevent the delicate *nae* from floating up to the top of the water. The left hand was full of *nae* ready for planting. It took almost half a day for us inexperienced children to get the knack of planting, and what an aching back! I can still feel the mud between my toes squishing up and keeping us from advancing due to the strong suction created by the muddy rice paddy. Day after day, for almost twenty days, we planted rice until the rice farmers completed the task. We felt proud that we had some part in the effort. We were given some sweet potatoes to take home. That was a real treat.

After the war, the mechanical rice-planting machine was invented. Rice planting and harvesting were done with ease. One man, on the machine for one day, was doing the task that used to take many people many days to accomplish.

Helping My Sick Classmate

My first year in high school was a very happy time. The newly built building still released the pungent aroma of spruce and pine. Our desks were new and the blackboard sparkled. The ocean breeze gently came across a large school yard surrounded by pine trees, which shielded the harsh winter wind blowing off from the Pacific Ocean. We could look out from the upstairs window to see ships on the ocean gliding into the Shin-Wakaura harbor.

The all-girls high school was named Bunkyo Jogakko. The Chinese characters Bun meant "words or letter." The second character Kyo meant "to study." Because it was a newly erected school, we had fairly young teachers in their late twenties or early thirties. No old fogies, so to speak. The principal was in his late forties. All of us were very happy and felt privileged to have such a nice atmosphere to really put our minds to work. The usual three Rs were taught and in addition we had geography, history, music, and PE. A special class of learning the classical Chinese was added. The subject was like a foreign language because it was all written in *kanji* (Chinese characters) and had a very special way to read it.

It was a very difficult class, and we really did not enjoy it. However, the teacher was very clever. He spent the last fifteen minutes reading a fun book of love stories or a very scary ghost story. This type of teaching enticed the students to study hard so we could listen to the fun stories at the end of the class.

One day, we had an unusually difficult lesson, and at the end, the teacher was reading a very scary ghost story. It was quite a long story, and as he read with soft voice leading to the crescendo, we were so frightened we held our desks so tightly that our knuckles turned white.

It was so quiet we could have heard a pin drop. Just then, an enormous roar, like a wounded animal, sounded, and the girl who sat across from me started to bang her head on her desk. All the girls screamed and ran out of the classroom. The teacher was so stunned that he stood frozen with the story book still in his hand.

My adrenaline rushed through my body, and instinctively, I knew my classmate needed help. I rushed toward her and held her head so it would not bang so hard. She was quite large for a Japanese girl and weighed more than I did. She was frothing at the mouth and her whole body was shaking by this time. I had never seen a grand mal seizure before, but I told myself to be brave and held her body while she slid off her chair. Now she was on the floor, and it was easier to hold her head in my lap, making sure she was not biting her tongue. By now, the teacher came to his senses and helped me turn her sideways and held her flailing arms so she did not bang them on the desk next to her. He then went to get another teacher next to our classroom to help him care for my friend. Two minutes seemed like an eternity as she shook. Finally, she stopped shaking, took a very deep breath, and fell into a very deep sleep.

Dead silence came across the classroom. When I looked around, all the rest of our classmates were peering through the window from outside the corridor, not saying a word. I could see only their big black eyes as big as saucers peering.

Later, when it was all over, I returned home to tell my father what had happened at school. He told me that my classmate had a grand mal seizure because she either forgot to take her medication or the story the teacher was reading was so scary that it stimulated her brain enough to trigger her seizure. Later, in nurses' training, when we were learning about seizures, I looked back to that very scary day. Now I realize that even at that young age, my desire to help sick people was already in motion.

Japan's Aggression

With the worldwide Industrial Revolution came the need to procure more natural resources such as iron, oil, and rubber. Remember, rubber substitutes like plastics were not yet developed when we were growing up.

Japan was rapidly becoming an industrial nation with very limited natural resources and was always looking to expand her territory.

Long before I was born, Japan was at war with different nations in order to get more iron to build ships or rubber for tires, etc.

For example, from 1894-1895, in the war with China in dispute over Korea, Japan won the war to gain control over Korea. Japan went to war with Russia in 1904-1905, and after defeating the Russian navy, Japan gained dominance over Manchuria. Japan went to war with China again in 1937 to get a free hand over Korea and some area of China. Always winning the war, Japan kept expanding her territory. September 27, 1940, Japan formed a military alliance with Germany and Italy and later attacked Indo-China to further gain more territory rich with natural resources.

As children, my sister and I were often among the spectators of a victory celebration parade for one war or another, not quite understanding the true meaning of why we were shouting, *"Banzai, Banzai"* (long live the emperor) while we waved a small Japanese flag with our friends.

Just to let you know, my Japanese grandfather, Sakinji Uehara, fought in the Russian-Japanese war that started in 1904 and received a medal for serving in the war. The medal is in the possession of my sister's son, Jay.

Pearl Harbor Day

The August of 1941, Kazue, nine years, Natsue, eleven years

We did not know WWII was just around the corner.

Needless to say, this subject is very emotionally painful and difficult for me to discuss. December 8, 1941, in Japan (December 7 in America) is unforgettable for anyone, but especially for me and for my sister Anne, it was the day our father's country and our mother's country starting to fight each other. What a shock to hear the radio blasting something about Pearl Harbor in Hawaii.

I was only eleven years old and my sister was only nine; no wonder we could not comprehend the seriousness or the magnitude of the war. As far as I can remember, Japan was always in conflict with some other country far away from us. We never thought anything about it until now. This time it became very serious. We all felt like a big bomb just exploded near our home, and all of us were about to be crushed beneath the rubble.

Thank God, we had a loving and very stable Christian home. Both parents together gathered us and told us it was very unfortunate that Japan chose to attack America and that neither Father nor Mother could explain the impact of this war to either side of the family. Needless to say, any news from our American family in Georgia stopped very abruptly.

Our parents were very strong in their Christian faith, and they both instilled in us the philosophy of trust in God and do your best in life, which has remained with us throughout our lives. I know now that the strong reassurance from our parents kept us children calm and on a steady path.

Now I look back and understand the war with America and the war in the Pacific were not about racism or because Japanese were different. The two nations had equally justifiable grievances against each other. To borrow the words from Victor Davis Hanson, who wrote for the *San Jose Mercury News* on April 12, 2010, "The brutal Pacific war was about ending an expansionary Japanese fascism that sought to destroy all democratic obstacles in its path."

I agree totally with Victor Hanson. The Japanese military's misguided greed led to the tragic end of Hiroshima and Nagasaki atomic bombing with many lives lost. I only hope and pray that peace without war will be possible in the near future.

WWII

After the war began, Japanese housewives started to gather and hoard materials for kimonos, shoes, socks, underwear, and other clothing needed for their families. Apparently, my father's nurses talked my father into stocking up on medical supplies such as bandages, gauze, and bats of cotton to make pressure bandages and some disinfectants that would have no expiration date.

Japanese doctors did not have antibiotics in those days; you see, penicillin was not yet discovered, and we were lucky to have some sulfa drugs. Since the Japanese military had confiscated most of the drug supply in order to treat their wounded soldiers in the Pacific, civilian physicians were left with almost nothing.

Our mother saw no need, or was unaware of the need, to stock up on some essentials and did not do so. Because of that, I have another story to tell later.

After the second year at war, I remember most of the confectionary shops started to close their doors for lack of sugar, chocolates, and vanilla, which all had to be shipped in from foreign countries. Some brown sugar was still available at times, but that too soon disappeared from the market shelves. By the third year, even salt and soy sauce were getting to be a rare commodity. Finally, the Japanese government imposed the food rationing system called *haikyu* in 1942. The town was divided into small sections, and each section had not more than one hundred homes. Each section of homes had a section called *tonarigumi*, which meant "group of neighbors." Each section head was responsible for circulating notices of any importance. It could be the dates of distributing soy beans or soy sauce, salt or dried bananas. Sometimes it would be miso paste or dried fish. Everyone started a so-called victory garden because all available young and middle-aged men were drafted into the army or the navy, and no able bodies, other than the very young and old, were left to fish or tend the rice fields.

My father rented a small triangular plot from a land owner who was our friend long before the war so my mother could plant her magnolia tree. Each year, the tree grew, and by 1940, it was so big its branches covered half of the triangle plot. Mother, my sister, and I planted our victory garden near the well on the other side of the magnolia tree so we could water our vegetables without having to walk too far from the well. The garden was fenced with a four-foot wire fence with a gate that opened close to our house. At first, everything went well, a perfect organic garden, and we were able to harvest pumpkins, sweet potatoes, tomatoes, and other green leafy vegetables; but as the war worsened and food was nowhere to be found unless you grew it yourself, there was none. About that time, someone started to steal our vegetables at night, and in the morning, we would find the vegetables half gone or the long-awaited, almost-ripened tomatoes yanked off the vine. It was very discouraging to us to see them gone; not only that, but the other vegetables were also left crushed under the robber's foot. Of course, the robbers could not come with a flashlight to see what they were picking. Sad, how hunger affected different people in different ways.

Toward the end of the war, one started to look for grass and eatable wild plants growing in the mountains.

I remember we heard that sweet potato vines could be eaten after we cooked them or parboiled them for a few minutes to take away the bitterness. Then we could change the water, this time to add salt and other flavors we wanted to add. Only after painstaking preparation could we eat the vine. I'm certain by that time, all the vitamins and minerals were bleached out and only fiber remained. But it filled our stomach and somehow killed our hunger. I learned to eat chickweed, wild mustard greens, and dandelions. Young chickweed is quite tender and sweet tasting.

Here is the other story I said I would tell you. Nothing seemed to change immediately after December 7, 1941. The first year, Japan's military was busy invading the Philippine Islands and other islands in the South Pacific. The shipping lanes were still open, though, and many basic supplies such as sugar, salt, rice, bananas, oil, fish, and cotton were easily available. Then we noticed in the second and beginning of the third year that to purchase these foods, you had to know the shopkeeper really well before you could buy sugar, soy sauce, salt, and candy, paying black market prices called *yami*.

The military, through the *tonarigumi*, started to collect iron and copper pans and pots, anything made from iron. Even iron flower vases were solicited (coerced is more like it).

I remember one day, a huge military truck piled high with pots and pans appeared in the small open area near our home. Any items that were iron, copper, or aluminum were taken away.

Since we had several large *okama* (iron porridge pots to cook rice), we donated the old one and kept the newer one for our use. An iron teakettle and a few iron and copper vases were donated.

Shoes and anything that had leather or rubber disappeared from the shop windows. Again, we started to feel the crunch.

In junior high, we were taught to sew. I mean really seriously sew our own blouses, jackets, and pants. We were taught to measure ourselves and make patterns from newspaper to fit ourselves.

When materials were no longer available at the shops, we started to use anything that we had in our home like old kimonos, curtains, and sheets. Father had two winter coats and a Japanese *manto* (cape) to go with his men's kimonos. Anne and I were given Father's cotton Yukata kimono to take apart and convert into a *monpe* (wartime girl's pants) because skirts were not worn toward the late war years. Father's *manto* made a warm winter jacket for us. They were all hand stitched by me or my sister. Since thread was not to be found anywhere, we unraveled the kimono. We did it in a fashion that saved long strands of thread that could be saved and reused. That was the only way we could make clothes.

Uniform made from kimono

When our shoes with rubber soles were no longer wearable because our toes were coming through the rotten material, we cut the rotten canvas off and kept the rubber soles. We reused it by sewing on another top and carefully attaching the sole to the newly fashioned shoe top.

We did not throw anything away, we reused things. Now the word is *recycle*. Ours was *reuse for survival*.

It took until 1948, the post-war years, before materials started to reappear in the shops. We had to make our own clothes. When the occupation forces came, my mother was able to get some spools of thread from the American military personnel. We were able to use the old foot-driven Singer sewing machine my mother had. It took quite a bit of thread for the bobbin. We were delighted to get new thread that would not break because it was getting old and rotten.

Years later, in the nurses' dorm at Emanuel Hospital, in Portland, Oregon, when I was doing my practicum in nursing, I had some time on my hands and sewed skirts, dresses, and blouses for my roommates to make some spending money. Sewing with Simplicity or Butterick dress patterns was such an easy task when you only had to fit the pattern to the body to take out or take in a larger seam. I had a lot of practice by the time I was married and had my own child and, later, my grandchildren for whom to sew. When I was living in Fullerton, California, I sewed for my neighbors. I even sewed the gowns for Ms. Fullerton, who lived behind our home.

Looking back, what started as a necessity turned into a wonderful hobby.

Digging the Tunnel

I remember when I was thirteen years old in the summer of 1943, my school cancelled summer vacation, and all children were sent up to the highest point around our town. This was through Mikazura, where the famous Kimiidera Buddist Temple stood, and after climbing many hundreds of steps straight up, we reached the famous temple.

Kimiidera Temple steps

There stood the Japanese army soldiers waiting for us. They took us around the mountain where we saw a large cave being excavated out of the side of the mountain. We were told to shut our mouths and just work, taking a large basket of red clay dirt and shale out of the tunnel. The soldiers would pile big boulders into our bamboo baskets. Two girls would shoulder the bamboo pole holding the basket, carry it out of the tunnel, and throw it over the side of the mountain, repeating the work all day. We were told when to break for water and have ten minutes of rest before getting up to repeat the labor, day after day. This was not fun anymore. We all wished we were back in the classroom.

The soldiers instructed us to promise that we would not tell anyone that we were working at the tunnel, which was to house large guns to defend our coastline. Since Wakaura was a port town with an oil refinery to the south at Minoshima, it needed defending. The port at Wakayama and Wakaura was deep enough to allow battleships to lay anchor. We saw Japanese navy ships come into port to load provisions. I really don't know, to this day, whether my parents knew about the military digging tunnels in the mountain near our home. My parents never questioned what this thirteen-year-old was doing during the summer vacation. We just came home exhausted and covered with red clay dirt.

I must have learned the real meaning of the words Silence is Golden.

Kimiidera Temple pagoda

Mitsubishi Factory

When the summer of 1943 ended without a vacation, we were happy and relieved to get back to school and start classes even if it was only a half-day session. This time, the air raids started and the B-29s were flying high in the sky, making a groaning sound on their way to Tokyo, Osaka, Nagoya, Yokohama, and other cities in Japan.

In the spring of 1944, my high school classes were held at the Mitsubishi factory grounds in the morning, and after lunch, we went to work at the factory. After my fourteenth birthday in August 1944, all my classmates were instructed to wrap very thin wires around a coil to make the spark coil for the engine in the Mitsubishi Zero plane for the Japanese Army Air Corps. The factory was huge, but the area we were assigned to was a very long room with long tables in the middle and chairs on each side for the girls to sit and wrap the porcelain spark coils. After we wrapped the layer of wire, the coil would be dipped into a vat of melted lacquer. The fumes from the hot lacquer were overwhelming in the summer and made the factory very uncomfortable from the heat. After many layers of wire and lacquer, the coils became so heavy they were difficult to lift and hold to work on them. We were only fourteen, and our hands were not big or strong. My sister was two years younger, so she was only twelve and remained in school for the morning session and went to the fields in the afternoon.

I worked very hard with the rest of my classmates. We were not allowed to speak to one another unless we needed help. Cranking the large mesh wire pan filled with coils down into the hot lacquer required help. This factory was very large and had many rows of work area like ours. Young women older than we, nineteen or twenty, came from Okinawa to work shoulder to shoulder with us. Sometimes, they would help lift the heavy pans of coils and pull the cumbersome crank to lower the coils into the boiling vats of lacquer.

One day, one girl was not strong enough to handle the crank by herself, so one end of the pan got tipped lower than the other side. Before we could yell at her to watch out, all the coils fell out of the pan one by one into the vat. We all screamed and ran to help her fish the coils out with very long tongs. It was a wonder no one got burned. Even now, I still shudder when I think about it; it was so scary.

A young army lieutenant, with highly polished leather riding boots and riding switch in his hand, would walk very slowly through each row of work benches. He must have been in his twenties. All the Okinawa girls were talking about how handsome he was but were working feverishly when he came through our aisles. We were too young to notice how handsome he was. We were too frightened when he would appear on our aisle because he would switch the riding whip against his boots, making a sound that would make us cringe. He would do this very slowly with each step he took. We did not dare to look up or even make a peep until he was far away from our work area.

I remember there were no foremen or factory workers to assist us young girls, only that one army officer going up and down the aisles every day. Toward the end of the war, there was nothing to work on. The once-plentiful supply of coils and copper wire dwindled. We would not work to wrap wire on the coils until the officer appeared at the end of our aisle, and then we would make it look like we were all working diligently. He must have known himself that we had nothing to work on. He never said anything to us, just walked endless miles up and down the factory aisles.

The American bombing raids became more frequent during the fall of 1944. Sometimes, our small town was bombed when the B29s would have leftover bombs to release on their way out of Osaka. They seemed to be dropped randomly to get rid of them before their return to base.

The air raid sirens shrieked often now and most of us had to run for cover in a *bokugo* (shelter)—a sandbag stacked dugout reinforced with thin planks. It would barely keep the shrapnel from coming through the shelter but would not hold up to a direct hit. When the siren sounded, we would stop working and run for our assigned shelter. To this day, the sound of a siren gives me a very queasy feeling in my stomach.

The U.S. military invaded Okinawa on April 1, 1945. This was the last stronghold offensive position of the Japanese Empire, which stood in the way of a U.S. assault on the mainland.

One day in late June 1945, I arrived for work to find all the girls from Okinawa crying. Their eyes were swollen and red. We asked, "What happened?" and were told that some parts of Okinawa fell to the Americans. Later, we were told that American forces secured the total island by July 2, 1945. The girls did not know if their parents and family were alive or not. After a few days, the word came that many natives in Okinawa had committed suicide by first pushing their children and then jumping themselves off the rocky cliff despite the fact that the American military personnel had assured them that they would be treated kindly. I am convinced that the Okinawans thought the Americans would treat them just like the Japanese military had treated their prisoners of war as they had witnessed many times in the past. What a tragic end to civilians consumed with fear.

We will learn later that five thousand civilians died at Itoman Village in Okinawa. Japanese military lost four thousand five hundred men during the eleven days of brutal carnage. On June 16, 1945, Navy Admiral Ota, in charge of defending Okinawa, died in a cave by committing suicide. Things got very grim from then on. The Americans were at our doorstep, only 350 miles away from Japan.

The Mitsubishi factory, where I worked, was bombed one morning. It sounded like the building was crashing down on our heads. After the bomb was released, it made a little whistling sound, then the blast came and big clouds of smoke rose. Soon after, the fire broke out, touching off more explosions. I sat in the shelter petrified and unable to move. The girls clung together with fright. Some began to cry, but no one panicked because we were told to stay in our assigned shelter until the "all clear" siren sounded.

When it ended, we all came out and surveyed the damage. Half of the factory was flattened, but the side where we girls worked was untouched. That day, the foreman and our teacher let us go home early. There was chaos around us with water, smoke, and rubble. It was dangerous for us to linger on.

My parents heard about the bombing of the Mitsubishi factory, not knowing whether I was injured or dead. They were very happy and relieved to see me come home. Apparently, on the same day the factory was bombed, the Bunkyo Jogakko was strafed by American planes.

We knew the Japanese military occupied one-half of our school building. So the Americans, gunning for the military, sprayed bullets all over the school yard. My sister, Anne, was in one of the fox holes they had dug to protect themselves. She told me she squatted to make herself look like a ball in a hole. She could not see the planes come or go, but she could hear the awful diving sound it made and heard bullets passing over her head. Then she heard a moaning sound next to her in the fox hole, but she was unable to see what happened until later when the "all clear" signal was sounded. Everyone emerged from the fox hole. One girl, the one moaning next to Anne, didn't make it out of the fox hole. She was gravely injured and taken to the hospital. This horrific experience was a very close encounter for my sister, Anne, only twelve years old. I was happy that God spared my sister that day.

After my sister emerged from the fox hole and looked at her school and came home, she told us that the school building was full of bullet holes. It was a good thing no one else in her class was injured.

Georgia Peach and Pecans

As you may recall, my mother's roots go back to the state of Georgia. She was the eldest of eight children. But four died in infancy. I had one aunt called Lillian and two uncles, James and Charles. I was named after my aunt because I was born on her birthday. I was told the uncles were born when Mother was near college age. The only Fulghum official family photo hangs on the wall of my living room.

Mother used to call herself a Georgia peach. The state of Georgia is famous for peaches and pecans. I never saw pecans shelled or in the shell until my grandmother, Matilda Fulghum, sent pecans at Christmas. We were in kindergarten at that time. If one lived in the USA, walnuts and pecans were commonly used in homemade cookies and candies. However, if you lived in Japan, it was an imported item, and unless you were a candy maker, no Japanese recipes called for pecans. My mother would tell us how they harvested pecans from trees in their backyard and put them out to dry. I could hardly wait until Christmas season to receive another package with the ever-famous pecans. The boxes of pecans stopped very abruptly when WWII began. How sad it was to never hear anything from our grandmother in America for almost five years.

Pre-WWII photo of Matilda Fulghum

During WWII, food became scarce and no sugar or candy was available; I frequently dreamed about the pecans and the homemade fudge from my grandmother.

After WWII, Grandmother, now in her late eighties, and my aunt Lillian, a severe diabetic, were unable to do the task of packing and mailing the gifts at Christmastime. That was okay with us because we were growing up and understood the circumstances.

Tonarigumi and Haikyu

When food became scarce, about one and one-half years into the war, the Japanese government organized a neighborhood information group. Each city was divided into small sectional districts and the districts divided into small sections of houses clustered together. Twenty to twenty-five homes were called *tonarigumi* (meaning "group of neighbors"). Each head of household took turns selecting a *kumicho* (a leader) to circulate information vital to "our defense." We would gather together and practice firefighting or helping people out of burning homes, etc. Firefighting was a bucket brigade, dipping water from the nearby pond. We also had a morning-exercise group with a roll call because it was felt that everyone needed to keep his/her stamina, agility, and endurance to run and walk. This was required in case the transportation service ceased to exist due to bombing with all the streets torn up. Actually, *tonarigumi* helped to bond neighbors together and grow unity, disseminate information, and develop the willingness to help one another. *Tonarigumi* was such a good idea that it continued into the post war, and much to my surprise, it is still an ongoing practice.

Another function of the *tonarigumi* was to distribute food equally to the citizens according to the number of people in each household. When food became scarce and hunger overcame us, human nature, or shall I say, the animal in each of us, caused us to think only about ourselves. I remember most of the shopping centers closed doors due to lack of commodities. Toward the end of the war, even though we lived by the sea, there were no fishermen left to catch fish. Men were all in the military fighting in the South Pacific. Any fish that reached our table was caught by some patient's family.

Surprisingly, there was plenty of butter and cream. Japanese cooking was void of butter, cream, or milk, and only the fancy Western style restaurants used butter to cook. Mother was elated that she could make her waffles each morning with butter and have cream in her English tea.

Mother was allowed to have flour for her portion of the food allotment. However, the so-called flour was unbleached and full of weevils. I used to watch her sift the flour to rid the weevils before she could bake her waffle in a very seasoned old-fashioned waffle iron. She guarded that iron with her life. I guess that waffle iron symbolized the only connection at this time to her mother country.

During the beginning of WWII, shipping routes were not disturbed, so fresh fruits like bananas, apples, tangerines, and oranges were plentiful, but when the transportation throughout Japan was disrupted, everything stopped. *Tonarigumi* had to distribute what little we had such as rice, potatoes, salt, white sugar at first, then brown sugar and, later, no sugar or salt. We received dried seaweed and small dried fish at times.

One day after school, I was asked by my father to stand in line for whatever food the *tonarigumi* were distributing. Usually, Father sent our Japanese nurse, *Miyo*, to receive food. However, this time, my father's clinic was so busy he could not spare her.

I carried my basket and stood in line. I noticed someone pointing fingers at me and whispering loudly so I could hear "that *ainoko* is here" (meaning "that half-breed is here"). That comment was not necessary, but they intended to hurt my feelings.

I ignored the comment and kept standing until I was next in line to receive our family portion of dried fish. Much to my amazement, the man measuring dried fish looked up and told me to go back to the end of the line. I had no choice but to obey him. After all, I was in my early teens, and he looked like he could bite my head off.

First, I felt angry that I had stood in line almost an hour like everybody else, and now I'm at the end of the line again. I knew if I complained I would encounter a worse fate. My family needed this food. I was at this man's mercy.

My family did not know what had happened that it took so long for me to return home from this task. After they heard my story, my father felt so bad for me and apologized. He said that since his Japanese nurse had no such experience, he thought nothing of it than to send me for the task. I was never asked or sent again to encounter such racially motivated blatant abuse.

Most people were malnourished. I remember fainting one day on the middle school parade ground listening to a speech the principal was making. My stomach was growling with hunger because, that morning, I had only a small bowl of rice porridge cooked with a small amount of sweet potatoes. I did not "come to" until a few minutes later after two teachers carried me into the caretaker's cottage on the school ground.

Some patients took pity on my family and brought food from their own farm. My father exchanged his medical services at times for food to sustain us. We all knew hunger; no one escaped it.

Mother and Kempei
(Japanese Military Police)

Long before the war, mother was asked to teach English at the Wakayama Police Academy. She gladly taught it without compensation and enjoyed the relationship she developed with her students. Uehara Sensei (Teacher Uehara) was well-known throughout the prefecture. The police department in our city knew all about us, and we had no fear. My father was well-known as an established physician, and people from as far away as Osaka came to his clinic to be treated for psoriasis. The name of my father's clinic was Emmanuel Clinic. My parents chose this name, walk with God, from the Bible. My parents wanted to dedicate my father's clinic to God, so he could ask for wisdom and guidance in healing people in need. The townspeople called my father's clinic *In maru-san.* (Immanuel-*san*)

The Japanese Military Police, called *Kenpei*, came into our lives uninvited, but looking back, under the circumstances and place in our lives at that time, the experience I'm about to tell you was unavoidable and unique, to say the least.

Our mother, being a past American citizen, was marked to be a possible security risk by the Japanese military. As the World War deepened, they sent a letter to our home, stating that each time Mother planned to travel out of our city, she was to report to the *Kenpei* and get permission. Thus, even though she was a Japanese citizen, she had to report each time she traveled to Osaka to her dentist for the treatment of her pyorrhea (a severe gum disease), probably caused by her lifelong diabetes and malnutrition.

Whenever Mother went to her dentist, she would take one of us girls for companionship, and also, just in case her diabetic condition worsened, we could get help for her.

Every trip we took, which was often because of complications in treatment, I could not help but notice a well-dressed man in his thirties seemed to follow us on the train to Osaka and back. Occasionally, I saw the same man following us into a restaurant, but he took a table far away from us. Then he followed us back onto the train; sometimes I spotted him on the edge of the platform smoking a cigarette. Even to a young teenager, it was obvious we were being followed. When I asked Mom about this person, she looked at me very calmly and said, "Oh, he is a plainclothesman making sure we are going where we said and back." She also felt perfectly safe because he would protect us in case of a problem. What kind of problem, she did not explain. Thank goodness that remained to be seen.

Soon, the city of Osaka was devastated and the dental office was destroyed with the city. Mother was unable to see her private dentist and had to find a suitable dental clinic in town.

Hiroshima and Nagasaki

The story of Hiroshima and Nagasaki "*Pika-Don*" (flash-loud noise)
The historic facts about the atomic bomb and the destruction it produced are well documented and easily accessible to anyone who wants to read about it. The story I'm about to tell is based on what we heard and experienced ourselves in Japan during WWII.

The propaganda machines of WWII Japanese military government were well oiled, cranking out lies most of the time, even though we were about to lose the war. They did not report the truth or the obvious. Thus, when the atomic bomb was dropped on August 6, 1945, at 8:15 a.m. on Hiroshima, nothing horrendous was reported. The newspaper reported that there was apparently a new type of bomb with destruction capabilities several times more than the usual bombs.

If people were close enough to see the bomb flash and hear the noise (*pika-don*), they were killed, and the intense heat created had far more capability of devastation.

By the end of the war, Germany shared the secret of rocket science with Japan and was sending the much-needed heavy water and uranium ore. Of course, Japanese military (the army and the navy) were experimenting in nuclear fusion and trying to make a nuclear bomb, but due to the lack of uranium ore, together with some needed scientific experiments, they were way behind the USA. This information was top secret so none of this was known by the civilians like us.

The news of a second atomic bomb falling on August 9, 1945, came one day before my birthday. We still did not realize the tremendous impact this bomb had on the future of Japan. We were all ready to fight until the end. Due to lack of information, most Japanese did not realize how horrific this so-called nuclear war was, which could bring about long-lasting effects.

August 6, 1945, *pika-don* killed and injured at least 140,000; three days later, at Nagasaki, 60,000 lost their lives. Not until much later did we learn about the long-lasting suffering of people with radiation illness, cancer (especially leukemia), and other diseases became clear.

The atomic bombs saved many more lives on both sides, bringing about a quick end to the WWII.

Little did I know that I would indirectly experience the devastation when the Chenoble Russia atomic fuel plant did a meltdown in the 1990s that caused multiple deaths by radiation and devastated the entire town.

It was the summer of 1949 when I learned that I was accepted into Lewis and Clark College in Portland, Oregon, as a foreign student with a full scholarship. My father took me and my sister, Anne, to visit our grandparents, Sakinji (grandfather) and Toku (grandmother), who lived in Fukuoka, Kyushu Island. I had not seen our grandparents since I was small and remembered their small house nestled next to a hill with a large lake filled with millions of tadpoles. They lived in the country, so there were no fences between the house and the rice paddies.

Our nurse cooked several hard-boiled eggs and packed some rice balls, called *onigiri*, with seaweed wrapped around them for each of us. We each packed a change of clothing in our backpacks and carried our own canteen of Japanese tea. From Wakayama, we changed trains at Osaka and boarded the train to Kyushu. There was no such thing as reserved seats or a Pullman car where one can stretch out to sleep. Those days, all the trains were coal-burning steam engines, and the smoke billowed. Since there were no seats available, we stood for twelve hours packed like sardines. It was very hot and humid, so all the windows were opened, but when the train entered a tunnel, the smoke came inside and everyone sneezed or coughed until we were back in fresh air again.

I don't remember how many times we had to repeat this uncomfortable experience of going through the tunnel, but we were glad that we got on the train. There were some people left at the station unable to get a foothold on the train, let alone board.

I remember standing on one foot and then the other for that long trip. We ate hard-boiled eggs and the onigiri. Oh my, it was so good. When we got thirsty, Father told us not to drink too much tea because we were packed so tight that we could not move to walk to the WC to relieve ourselves. So for twelve long hours, we stood held up by some other person next to us.

Just before Hiroshima, the train stopped, and the conductor told the passengers to close the windows and put the blinds down. We were not to look at the devastation.

When we slowed down to pass the Hiroshima station, I was fortunate to be standing between two cars connected together with corrugated canvas, and there were no curtains to pull down. I could see that nothing was there but a burned-out platform, charred and crumbled rubble, no green trees, only occasional sticks of something standing here and there. The red bricks had melted and looked corrugated.

It certainly did not look like our town that was burned by fire caused by the falling incendiary bombs. Nothing was standing here, not even a charred telephone pole. As far as my eyes could see, it was devastation personified.

I whispered to myself, "So this is what *pika-don* did."

Wakayama City Bombed

Early in 1945, the B29s would fly over our town from the ocean toward Osaka and Nagoya and back again. We did not experience any actual bombing. Shimotsu, the city a few kilometers south of Wakayama, had gas and oil refineries. These facilities were bombed one night. That was our first experience of how horrific the exploding tanks sounded and always at night. As children, we were very frightened to see flames lighting up the night sky. It looked and sounded like the explosions were right behind our home. Actually, they were over a small mountain away and across the bay.

The most devastating air raid to Tokyo came on March 10, 1945, when 334 B29s dropped bombs simultaneously and flattened the city. The night of July 9, 1945, Wakayama was bombed and we totally experienced the war. The air raid siren sounded after we went to bed, but we were used to hearing the planes go over our heads on their way to the big cities, so we thought nothing of it and went to sleep. This time it was different; we could hear the noise from the incendiary bombs flashing. Bombs were falling along the Kinokawa River, separating Osaka prefecture and Wakayama prefecture.

Wakayama Castle

I'm certain the B29s' bombsights were focused on the river first and then saw the beautiful Wakayama Castle. The castle was on a hill called Tora Fusu Yama, named for being in the shape of a tiger lying down with its paws stretched out. The castle had one large moat around it with a large camphor tree at the main entrance.

Camphor tree

This tree was over three hundred years old and was planted by the *Tokugawa Daimyo* (feudal lord) when the castle was first built. The townspeople designated this tree as a sacred tree signifying that the tree god and his/her spirit resided in this tree. The trunk was three to four yards around. I'm certain that even with the air raid black outs, sirens sounding and all the lights turned off in the castle, the white walls of the castle were not difficult to identify. In addition, the city of Wakayama was built in a circle around the castle. The large factories and military bases were toward the outskirts of the city.

The first large incendiary bomb was dropped on top of the castle. When the city perimeter was identified by the burning castle, the incendiary bombs started to fall, the wooden homes started to burn from the castle outward and from the perimeter inward.

People in the city were trapped with nowhere to go. The heat was so intense that some jumped into the muddy water of the castle moat. I was told later that many people fell or were pushed into the moat. Some were trampled to death and some children drowned. Several days later, when I was reunited with my classmates who lived in the city, I heard that the temperature of the usually cold water rose to almost boiling because of the heat created by the burning city and the rocks surrounding the moat were heated up. It was difficult to imagine the horrific experiences the people must have had. Since we lived outside of the city, we could only hear the sounds and see the black smoke billowing and flames lighting up the night sky.

My father's medical clinic and our home next to the clinic were about twenty miles out of the city in an area called Wakaura-Guchi. The bus and streetcar lines split from there to go to Kainan and Shin Wakaura where the famous Japanese-style Ryokan hotels were. The Ryokans were lined up, hugging the picturesque shoreline. Among many, Okatoku-Ro and Bokai-Ro were the most elegant and beautiful of the three- and four-story hotels. Bokai-Ro, meaning "ocean view hotel," even had an aquarium built into the side of the cliff, displaying many unusual tropical fish. The temperature for a few miles around our town was similar to California and seldom had snow. The prefecture was noted for growing tasty oranges and tangerines. The warm Pacific currents lapped at our shores and made the area perfect for growing citrus fruits.

Wakaura Resort Hotels

This area was also famous for the sea shore resorts. Many poems were written about thirteen hundred years ago about the picturesque shoreline of Wakaura in the book of poems called *Manyoshu*.

Sea-viewing hall

The bombs were sporadic, and very few homes were burned around our neighborhood. Several large incendiary bombs fell on the *Seishin Byoin* (mental hospital) in front of our house on the hillside, and the wooden building burned profusely. The patients started to roam the streets unaware of the reasons why they were released. It gave me a very weird feeling. I saw a pale-faced female patient, about thirty years old, with long black hair down to her waist. She had a faraway vacant look in her eyes, in a dirty white robe, grabbing onto an eggplant bush. She was dragging it, eggplant roots and all, down the road. I took one look at her and gave her the right of way so she could pass me on her way to nowhere, aimlessly placing one foot in front of the other. She looked truly like a ghost.

The bombs kept falling closer to us. The smell of burning wood, flesh, and other unidentifiable smells permeated the air. My sister and I ran with the *bokuzukin* (thickly padded hat) on our heads to our dugout (*bokugo*) to get shelter, but it was full of strangers. I told them that this *bokugo* was ours and please go to your own. They said nothing and just ignored us, their faces covered with mud and soot.

I was very angry and, fearing for my own life, ran back to my house. While I was running through the living room to get to the stairs, I bumped against the French table with the cut glass top, which my mother cherished. The table toppled to the floor, crashing the glass top into a million pieces. I felt bad but could not do anything to put it back. My life was in danger. I raced up the stairs to our bedroom, which my sister and I shared; we had a double bed with a mattress. I cannot remember where my sister was, but she was nowhere to be found. I dragged the mattress all by myself down the steps and out the front door to our outer garden and hid under it for the remainder of the night.

The next morning, I tried to lift the mattress to take it back to our bed. I could not lift even the corner of it. I've heard stories of people having enormous strength in a time of need. The adrenaline must have been surging through my fifteen-year-old body, so I became Wonder Woman for a night.

The next day, after the air raid was over, the smoke and ashes driven by the wind blackened the morning sky. Even thirty miles out of the city, where we lived, the streets were dusty with fallen ashes. Many refugees came strolling into the suburb and through my community, going south to the cities of Kainan and Minoshima. I saw many of our friends. Some said they were separated from their parents but were old enough to know where to go, hoping to meet up with them later. My family offered them some water or tea to drink to quench their thirst before they continued their journey. I realized how fortunate that all my family were together and not even hurt. God really took care of us. I was filled with thankfulness and joy that somehow we survived this ordeal.

My father was not inducted into the military because he was married to an American and was considered a security risk even though my mother lost her American citizenship when she married my father. A vicious rumor started to circulate after the bombing of Wakayama that my mother directed the B29 bombers to the target by signaling with her flashlight. My father was the only available physician left in our town.

After the bombing for over a month, we did not see our father and our nurse other than taking clean clothing up to him at the beautiful hotels at the seashore, now converted to hospitals. Burned victims, injured, and sick occupied the rooms with their relatives helping dress the wounded and tending to the sick. My father was the only physician helping the sick and wounded. He said later that tetanus was the worst disease to combat because they had no vaccine. So he could not save some people even when he knew how.

Within a few days, the medical supplies my nurse had hoarded and saved before the war were gone. The once-beautiful hotel rooms changed into foul, smelly blood-soaked rooms. Everywhere my father looked, there were corpses lying without any people mourning their death. All my father could do was to instruct the able-bodied people left to carry the dead out quickly and bury them fast in the mass grave they dug near Kataonami, once a beautiful beach area, to prevent the spread of communicable disease.

The Aftermath and Human Suffering

The beautiful seaside hotels just a few blocks away from our house were immediately converted into hospitals for military and civilians alike. My father was in charge of all the patients, numbering thousands.

My mother, sister, and I were left to fend for ourselves. Before Father left to care for the wounded, we all gathered together to hold hands and pray—first, that God will grant wisdom and physical stamina for our father so he could exercise his knowledge as a physician to minister the injured and sick; second, that God will keep us safe while we were apart from one another.

After our good-byes, hugging and kissing him, we did not see our father for a few weeks. We did receive word by messenger that he was okay. The phone lines were all down, so that was the only communication we had. Those few weeks were a blur and total nightmare because the food supply was cut off, and even the small vegetable garden we had started was ransacked during the night by others searching for food. Anne and I were too young to realize then how difficult it was for our parents to keep us fed. No one was going out to catch fish; farmers were busy making enough produce for the military and their own families. There was no food left to sell. Whatever was left over was traded for other goods such as clothing, salt and miso paste for soup.

My father returned home only to rest for a while. Then he went back to the makeshift hospital at the hotels overlooking the beautiful sea. The only thing beautiful about it now was the clean fresh ocean air and the serene beauty of the unchanging seascape shimmering under the midsummer sun.

After a few days had passed, it became very apparent that there were not enough people to nurse the sick and the suffering. The Red

Cross-trained nurses were there but so few in number that they did not have enough hands to go around.

Bunkyo Jogakko organized available young girls, the ones still left able to help. The teachers took them up to the makeshift hospital in the hotels. My sister, Anne, was recruited.

Although the Mitsubishi factory was bombed and damaged, my workstation was operational, so I was ordered to return to the factory to resume work. Therefore, I knew nothing about the horrific duties my sister, Anne, was assigned to do. She told me much later in life that she tended to changing burn dressings of patients lying right next to one another in the order they came in. Patients young and old, male and female, next to one another without privacy, without bed linen, straight on the bare *tatami* mats. Some were lucky to have not-so-injured relatives tending to their needs. Babies were crying from hunger and thirst next to their dying mothers equally malnourished in delirium. Without adequate supervision, my sister, only thirteen at that time, worked diligently without rest from morning to dusk.

Of course, none of the so-called medical supplies were sterile; they were all made from torn-up sheets and towels found in the hotel. But they were clean. Soon, the buzzing flies laid eggs in the oozing wound and hatched. The maggots ate the dead flesh and cleaned the wound. It sounds gross to us now, but my father said, "Thanks to those flies, cleaning out the necrotic flesh that the doctors did not have time to clean, wounds started to heal." Now even in the USA, physicians sometimes use the so-called sterile maggots in wounds deep and difficult to reach.

Anne came home exhausted each night, hardly spoke to any of us, ate her supper, and went to bed only to repeat the same service like a robot, day after day. I had nothing but admiration for my young sister who so heroically and kindheartedly tended those sick and dying at such a young age.

My work at the Mitsubishi factory came to a slow stop because of the lack of supplies. Since the bombing, the roads were blocked and the supply convoy could not get through. We only sat at our workbench and talked to each other.

A few years later, when all the nightmares of the war were not so vivid, I asked my father about his most difficult task of caring for several thousand burned patients. My dad said that there was a severe shortage of tetanus vaccine and that only the young, who had a chance of recovery, would get the injection. Without a blink, he said, "I hated to decide who would get the tetanus injection to prevent lockjaw and who would die from not receiving the preventive medicine. That kind of decision should be left to God and not for a physician doing his best to save lives."

A few miles down the hill, near the white sand beach lagoon called Kataonami, there was a massive grave dug to bury the unknown dead. We had to bury the dead fairly fast to prevent the dreaded communicable diseases under such chaotic circumstances. To this day, there are always fresh flowers placed at the site, commemorating the people who lost their lives in the unforgettable night when Wakayama was bombed.

The End of WWII

August 15, 1945

I will never forget the day when Emperor Hirohito spoke regarding Japan's unconditional surrender to the USA. It was five days after I turned fifteen.

On August 15, exactly at twelve noon, the broadcast started. The emperor's voice was almost wispy and, at times, shaky. This was the first time most Japanese heard his voice directly over the radio. Most of the time, we heard him on news reels staged for propaganda reasons. For those speeches, he spoke with words from classical Japanese language. This time, he spoke using the language commonly used in our daily communication.

I was still working at the Mitsubishi factory in Wakayama City and I heard the broadcast at the factory. My schoolmates and the girls from Okinawa were crowded into a very small tunnel-like hallway with one lightbulb swinging from the ceiling. It was a very dismal setting, to say the least. Everyone around me started crying.

I was with mixed feelings. I felt bad for my country losing the war. But my family suffered so much prejudice due to my mother being an American. Many times when I was walking down the street, I had to dodge rocks and stones flying toward me thrown by some children or insulting words spoken loudly by adults. I was truly happy that I no longer had to watch out for my safety as we commuted to the factory and back home.

That day when I returned home, my parents were waiting for us with smiling faces. They said that we were all safe now, and the American soldiers would not harm us. We all held hands and prayed together, thanking God because He kept us safe during the trying four years.

After the surrender was signed on September 2, 1945, on board the battleship *Missouri*, most townspeople thought the American occupation forces would inflict bad things on the Japanese, just like the Japanese military committed atrocities to the Chinese, Koreans, and the people of the Philippines when they conquered their countries. When the news came that the Americans were arriving, three quarters of the people in our small town closed shop, battened down their doors, and fled to the hills to hide. The small town of Wakaura was usually bustling with people but now was empty. Only an occasional stray dog or cat searching for food was found. It seemed like a ghost town for a week.

The American forces landed safely at the Shin Wakaura harbor, which was not mined by the Japanese military. The long line of weapon carriers and jeeps carrying military personnel passed through our town of Wakaura.

The first wave of soldiers was military police with their special helmets and armbands and machine guns perched on top of their jeeps. There were some foot soldiers that passed us, dressed in full gear that looked so heavy on their backs. My parents, my sister, and I lined up next to the street to watch them pass. Later, I was told that the marching GIs were all experienced soldiers who fought in the battle of Okinawa.

Much to my surprise, a company of black soldiers came marching up the street. I had never seen black people in my life, only in pictures. At first, because they were so big and tall and oh so black, I was frightened. They were all marching toward the old Japanese military barracks, the same barracks where my father had taken the cursory military training. The GIs would occupy the barracks for a few years.

Remember, U.S. military in 1945 was still segregated, and the company of black soldiers camped in tents near the Kinokawa river just beyond the burned-out city at the border of Wakayama and Osaka prefecture.

After that week of occupation forces landing, things were quiet and very peaceful. Most townspeople came back and welcomed the GIs.

The shopkeepers opened their shops to exchange Japanese goods for cigarettes and candy provided by the GIs.

Just for the sake of research, I was reading some articles and viewing documentary programs about WWII, and I found that President Truman knew about the possibility of Japanese surrender on August 11, but he waited to announce the end of the war until after the Emperor Hirohito announcement was made at noon on August 15.

Also, about that time, several Japanese military officers sought to carry out a coup d'état to kidnap the emperor at the palace grounds so that the surrender announcement would not be made on August 15 and determined the military would fight to the end. The plan was ironically foiled by an early-morning air raid on Tokyo, and without proper lighting of the interior of the Imperial Palace, it was impossible to find their way through the well-guarded palace grounds to find the emperor and confiscate the recorded message of surrender. After the foiled plan, the young officer committed suicide by facing the palace grounds and shooting himself in the head. In other words, he lost face big time.

Post WWII American Military Occupation Forces in Wakayama

The war had ended and somewhat chaotic peace has begun.

The year of Showa (1945) August 15, the war ended. Douglas McArthur arrived at Atsugi Airport on August 30, 1945. Also on the same day, the American navy arrived in Japan. On September 2, 1945, the Japanese surrender was signed on the USS *Missouri*.

The American armed forces General Headquarters (GHQ) was first established in Yokohama at the New Grand Hotel as the temporary established Occupation Forces Military Government.

On September 8, 1945, GHQ was moved to Tokyo. Occupation forces started to communicate with Japanese government.

September 11, 1945, General Hideki Tojo was arrested. Soon after, other Japanese high-ranking military members were arrested and, one by one, incarcerated, and later tried as a war criminal.

The first meeting of Emperor Hirohito and General Douglas McArthur took place on September 27, 1945. The most famous photographs of Hirohito standing next to General McArthur were taken that day of the first meeting. Two days later, on September 29, 1945, that photograph was published in the Japanese paper. After the first meeting, McArthur saw the emperor eleven more times. Japan's future was indeed on the shoulders of those two.

I called it chaotic times because so many changes had occurred. No matter where one looked, there was nothing in sight except for rubble of burned-out buildings, homes, and department stores.

Before WWII, Wakayama had two large department stores, one called Marusho and the other Takashimaya. The Marusho store was five stories high, which once stood very proudly at the entrance of Burakuricho. It now stood with its twisted steel frames sticking up into the heavens as though it were asking to be restored to its original grandeur decked with marble columns and intricately designed terrazzo flooring.

My sister Anne and I have fond memories of riding in an elevator operated by a smiling elevator attendant dressed immaculately in her uniform complete with hat, white gloves, and saying *irassaimase* (welcome). The large door to the elevator was a beautiful work of art of inlayed abalone shells with gold and silver designs of a beautiful landscape with peacocks spreading their wings. I felt like a princess when we were motioned to step in and ride up to the roof garden with lots of rides, a merry-go-round, and miniature golf. While Mother had tea and some dessert, my sister and I would play for hours and have fun. Those were the days when we knew nothing about wars and were able to spend our small childhood years in parental love and peace.

Our prestigious Wakayama Presbyterian Church, with its beautiful pipe organ, was also reduced to rubble. In its place, a small Quonset hut stood. My mother had a folding portable organ that she donated to the church, so at least we could sing hymns with accompaniment.

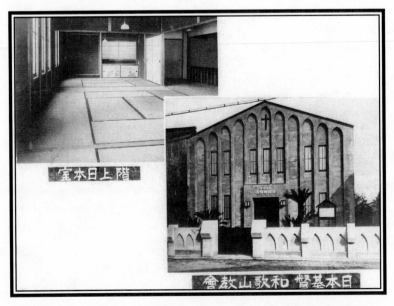

The meeting room and front view of the church before the bombing

Quonset hut church, Mother's english Bible class in 1947

The whole city had entered into the restoration phase, and many small trucks were busily removing rubble and unwanted materials to the dumpsite. I felt at least something was showing progress.

The occupation forces of General McArthur's military government teams were well established by 1946. The small but prestigious extension of its occupation forces was established in each prefecture throughout Japan.

The Wakayama American Military Government team personnel was small, but very efficient. It consisted of a colonel at the top, a captain at the head, a warrant officer, called Mr. O, motor pool corporal S, and two privates first class. One was a tall blond-haired nineteen- or twenty-year-old private first class, W. The other was a second-generation Japanese-American who enlisted in the army to act as an interpreter. However, the American captain soon found out the language the interpreter had learned as a child through his parents was full of dialect and a very poor quality. It was lacking many amenities or words that should be used in speaking to prefecture officials such as the governor, the mayor, or others.

The rest of the staff consisted of clerical support staff of American civilians; most of them were second generation Japanese girls in their twenties.

A few weeks past my high school graduation, I noticed a jeep was parked in front of my father's clinic. I thought nothing of it because my father often interpreted for the physicians of the Fifty-fourth Evacuation Hospital team stationed at the former Japanese military barracks. They were stationed there to repatriate the American soldiers captured by the Japanese military during the war and brought to Japan for forced labor. They were very sick from illness or malnutrition, often having been beaten or having encountered mental torture.

Most of the American soldiers captured were seasoned veterans and fought through the South Sea Islands. They were not young; and most of them were in their late twenties and their thirties with family waiting for them in the States, not knowing whether they were alive or dead until the war ended. The American Red Cross was "Johnny on the spot" after the war and was busy taking charge of notifying the families back in the States. Even my mother received word, through the American Red Cross, from my grandmother back in Macon, Georgia, that all was well and that her brothers and sister were relieved to know that my mother and her family all survived the war without a scratch.

The jeep I noticed at my father's clinic belonged to the American captain. He was visiting my father to ask him if his daughter Lillian could come to work for the military government team as a Japanese national to accompany the officers on their visitation trips to the Japanese governmental offices. The reason the captain gave my father was that the so-called official army interpreter's language skills were inadequate and often angered the Japanese officials by using the wrong words or leaving out their *keigo* (honorable words), which should be used to address them. I was told later, by my father, that the American captain pleaded to let me come to work for them even for a few months while I was free of schoolwork and before I must enter college the next spring.

The captain promised my father that I would be treated respectfully. The paperwork for me, a Japanese national working for the American military, took a while since I had to clear security checks.

Finally, the day arrived to report to my job. My official title was listed as clerk typist, and when I was not interpreting for the captain or other military personnel, I was taught to resend and amend military documents as they came in daily. I was quite busy with that task since no one had the time to do that type of so-called boring job, but to me it was a challenge and a chance to read English documents. I was learning the job quickly and well as Mr. O, the warrant officer with quite impressive hash marks up his sleeve, taught me other things to do. I learned to type with all ten fingers without looking at the keyboard. Later, when I went to college, I thanked my lucky stars that I had the opportunity to do so. I also learned to distribute the incoming mail and to collect outgoing mail. This freed the other personnel to do more pressing work. I never thought my job was mundane or boring because I was learning things I never had a chance to learn or do before. I took everything as a challenge. One never knew this type of work might come in handy someday. And it did later in life for me to keep my important papers filed correctly and to amend or resend insurance papers or other documents as they came in and not just left piled on my desk.

Mr. O was pleased that I learned quickly and retained what he taught me. He was a man in his forties, small stature, and with a very kind, matter-of-fact manner to teach others. I never heard or saw him get angry or be angry with anyone. Even the captain treated him with respect.

I told myself to mind my Ps and Qs. When I was working, I never stopped to talk to anyone unless people came to my cubicle to ask me something or give me more papers to file. I'm sure Mr. O approved of my work ethic because he could see me from his office. Even when I took my break, I was gone exactly fifteen minutes and no longer. Although I enjoyed talking to other girls in the office and made friends, I never was very close to anyone except my girlfriend Ms. J. Ms. J's father was a Japanese businessman in Australia before the war, and she was born and raised and went to grade school and high school in Sidney. She spoke with an Australian accent and was different from others. Her parents brought her back to Wakayama City to live with her grandparents to learn Japanese and learn the traditional Japanese culture. Ms. J came to my mother's English Bible class so she could speak English and enjoy some free time. Otherwise, her parents and her very strict grandparents kept a very close eye on her.

Ms. J kept saying, "I'm going back to Australia. I hate it here." I always felt sorry for her because she acted like a fish out of water and never wanted to accept anything to do with Japan or its culture. The only time she seemed happy was when she was working at the military government team speaking English, laughing, and joking with the *Nisei* civilians, second-generation Japanese, working as a clerk typist. I doubt that she had any male friends privately because she was nearing a marriageable age, and dating was arranged by her family.

A month passed fast, and somehow, by the grapevine, my father heard that I was doing fine at the military government team and that I was well liked by everyone, and there were no complaints from the Japanese officials about my Japanese word selection. I'm certain my father was relieved that I did well and that, so far, I did not disgrace the family name.

My duties sometimes extended into the evening hours. At times, I was invited to attend a banquet with Japanese officials and the American officers, of course, to interpret and act as a liaison. I felt it was an important post, and I felt quite comfortable in what I was able to do. You see, sometimes, the Japanese language has no words in English that can be directly translated. One can only translate the meaning. This is where the *Nisei* translators get stumped trying to find the suitable words.

Most of the conversation during the banquet was not of an official nature; it was a time of fun and relaxation. The Japanese officials would try to make the Americans drunk and only get tipsy themselves. I found that the Japanese cannot hold their liquor too well and always got drunk first.

When my father found out that I was going to interpret at these parties, he asked me to come to his clinic one evening. Much to my surprise, he had lined up on the table all the liquor: scotch, gin, vodka, and some Japanese sake. He told me since he cannot be at the banquet to protect me, I must learn how to drink sensibly. In other words, don't get drunk and always act as a lady, mindful of your station as an interpreter. He also told me I was working as an interpreter and not a guest although I was served the same food as the guests and was seated among the men delighted to have a pretty girl sitting next to them. I must be alert to my surroundings and the situations at hand.

Much to my mother's disapproval, the lesson of how to pace myself when drinking went on for almost two hours. My father told me always to eat before I attended these dinner meetings to coat my stomach and not to mix different liquor. I was always to stick with one kind of drink and sip it slowly. He kept asking me how my head felt or was I feeling woozy? As I told him how I was feeling, a slightly light-headedness feeling, he told me that this feeling will be my signal to stop drinking and rest, to eat more food, or to engage in more conversation.

My sister always accused me of coming home drunk because she smelled scotch on my breath. Now Japan's drinking age is twenty-one, but post-war Japan sixty-five years ago, they had no such limitation or drinking laws for minors.

One weekend, the captain invited one of his officer friends and his fourteen- or sixteen-year-old son to a picnic on the beautiful beach of Wakayama. Our town was famous for its white sand beaches that extend way into the sea without rocks or drop suddenly deep into the ocean. This weekend was to be a company picnic, and the army cook made potato salad and many different sandwiches. The captain called my parents to get permission for me to come along because he thought it might be fun for his friend's son to have a female companion at this outing.

I was pleased to be invited, and my parents allowed me to go. The jeep arrived on time with Corporal S as the driver. I was introduced to the young man whose face was covered with acne, and he had braces on his teeth. I had never seen corrective braces on anyone, so first I thought he was in a fight and some of his teeth were knocked out of his mouth and underwent some surgery. I had a feeling that he was coaxed to come. He did not seem very happy to see me or engage in pleasing conversation. I would say the young man would have liked it better if he was just left alone. However, I felt I should take the initiative and start a conversation. It was my mistake to ask him closed-ended questions. The boy answered me a short yes or no, without offering any other information; he was again silent.

It was apparent the boy was immature or very shy or, better yet, uninterested in a date with a Japanese girl. At any rate, I was frustrated and, to tell you the truth, very bored.

Thank goodness, when we got to the beach, we all went swimming. Since I was an excellent long-distance swimmer in high school and can stay in the ocean a long time without tiring, I enjoyed it very much.

Soon, we were called to eat and had a wonderful picnic lunch. The American-style chocolate cookies and fruit after lunch snack were delicious. This was my very first experience of a picnic American style and was very impressed with all the delicious food and the games we played.

We played volleyball, and I joined in the game, playing well. I did not tell anyone that I was on the volleyball team in high school. Some of the men started a poker game and seemed to enjoy what they were doing (laughing and joking), but that was gambling to me, and I stayed far away from that picnic table knowing especially that my mother would not approve of her daughter loitering near a gambling table.

Late that afternoon, some of the GIs said they were going back to their billet, and since it was getting to be close to dinnertime, I asked if I could hitch a ride home. They said yes, so without saying good-bye to the boy or the captain, I left with the two GIs and two other girls from the office.

My parents were all ears about what went on at the picnic, and I told them all about the delicious lunch and the chocolate chip cookies that were served and how we swam and played volleyball. I did not mention the poker game but told them I came home with two GIs and not with the party with whom I left.

My parents must have had some inside informer in the military government team because the word came back that I left the picnic without saying good-bye to the host or the boy. My mother told me she was embarrassed that I did not exercise my etiquette. I must say, my lack of social grace not to thank my host was not acceptable to my mother, a Southern belle, and this lecture from my mother stayed with me the rest of my life. Later, in America, I had a situation similar to this with a very boring date. I remained cordial and felt sorry for this man who did not know how to carry on a conversation.

Toward the end of 1949, the Japanese government, with its new constitution, was getting stabilized and no longer needed the Americans to hold their hands, so to speak. There were talks about this military government team to close by the end of the year. For me, it was bittersweet news. However, I was looking at taking my college entrance exam in February, and my sister urged me that I must at least review my books and put my heart into my studies. Doshisha University in Kyoto was a prestigious university and a popular one for students to apply.

My short but sweet experience with the American government team ended in December of 1949, and another chapter of my life story was to start soon.

The Datsun—Boron-San-Chan

Anne and the Japanese military Datsun

We own its license

Boron is an abbreviation for *Boroboro*, meaning "rags or old and worn-out." *San* is the word used after a name to honor people. *Chan* is used for children.

Boron-San-Chan is the nickname my sister and I gave to the small four-seat convertible Datsun my father purchased from the Japanese army surplus after the war. By 1947, everything military or civilian items belonging to the Japanese military had to be sold or scrapped.

Our father showed some interest in purchasing an automobile that was on the auction block. The Datsun had a newly made canvas convertible top, was painted a light blue, and looked so cute. It was formerly owned by a Japanese military officer and had to be disposed. No one drove or owned an automobile in 1947 unless they were in the business of transportation or happened to be a taxi driver.

Several American-born Japanese (*Nisei*) boys in their early twenties, who attended my mother's Bible class, encouraged my dad to get this small car. One young man, Mr. M, promised my father that he would teach my father how to drive and care for the car.

Since our home or the clinic had no garages, Father cut the outside fence next to the clinic and made a large door. Now he was able to drive the car from the side street into the yard next to his clinic. That became a carport without a roof.

Mr. M taught my dad and my sister to clean spark plugs and crank the car to start. My sister learned to be a mechanic, helping Father when he needed her to get in the car, shift into neutral gear, and pump the gas while he cranked the engine. I was impressed, but I guess I did not like to soil my hands with grease. Mother and I often rode in the car as passengers but never offered to help when the car gave a big cough, a jerk, and stopped. According to the sound of the engine, my father and sister would know if it was due to dirty spark plugs or bad gasoline. The gas my dad purchased was also army surplus and heaven only knows how old it was or who tampered with it. There were no official gasoline stands in our town.

Very soon after World War II, Wakayama prefecture, where we lived, widened the existing narrow roads, especially the streets within

Wakayama City. Now we had a wide four-lane boulevard with trees planted in the meridian or on either side of the sidewalk.

In 1947, the boulevard in front of the prefectural government buildings was paved and was an ideal place for my father to practice driving with Mr. M as a driving instructor. My father did well, but I can imagine that without power steering, even a small car was difficult to steer.

After a while, he felt comfortable to take us out for a ride. One day, Mother and I sat in the backseat with my sister in the front passenger seat as we all took off for a Sunday-afternoon drive on a scenic winding road toward the city of Osaka. I believe it was springtime, and the pink cherry trees were dotted along the mountainside. We were enjoying the picturesque scenery, but when we came around a bend, Father mishandled the steering wheel and the little Datsun promptly fell into the roadside ditch. Surprised but not hurt, we all got out while Father was trying to rock the car out of the ditch. The engine roared and the tires dug deeper into the soft clay.

Fortunately, a jeep with four American soldiers drove by and stopped because they saw my Caucasian mother and asked if they could help. Mother told them what happened. The GIs told us to stand aside and got off the jeep. With two in front and two in back of the Datsun, they gave a heave and promptly lifted the little car out of the ditch and onto the road. It was done with precision and grace. We were amazed at their strength. We thought they were Supermen. We could have been stuck for hours on a not-so-well-traveled road. When we thanked the GIs, they said, "No sweat." I had never heard those words and wondered why they would say that instead of "You're welcome." Mother told us later that "no sweat" was an American slang meaning "It was a simple task." It was so simple without too much effort that they did not even perspire. I learned another new expression.

Mother expected my father to have the Datsun in perfect running order. But contrary to her wishes, it often sputtered, choked, and came to a stop at the most inopportune time.

Often, we would be on an outing, and without warning, the little engine would cough, jerk, and come to a dead stop in the middle of the road. Mother would be so upset that she would take me and start walking toward the nearest train station or bus stop to catch a ride home. She would leave my sister and father "high and dry," expecting them to clean the spark plugs to get the car running again. That's why we nicknamed the Datsun *Boron-san-chan*, meaning Mr. Old and Decrepit.

The Summer of Decision Making

March 1949, I had just graduated from newly named Seirin Koto Gakko (high school). It was coeducational with one classroom divided in half: on one side sat the boys and the other side was for the girls. It was so strange that girls stuck together and the boys congregated in the same fashion. Neither group was comfortable to mix with the other. I was enjoying my first summer without any responsibility or care in the world and felt free as a bird.

Senior high graduation

That summer, my father asked me if I wanted to take the entrance exam next February to Doshisha University in Kyoto, Japan. Kyoto was the only town spared from bombing because the American government felt the city had an enormous Japanese cultural background and it was worth saving. Although I was told some bombs fell on the outskirts of the city, nothing was touched in the city proper.

My father was very wise and never pressured me to do anything I did not want to do. When he was young, he wanted to be a botanist, but because he was very bright and promising, he was pressured into medicine and became a physician. He did not regret that, but his true love was botany.

My parents also felt that I would do better in the United States because I was of a mixed race and could blend into the multicultural society better than the totally Asian culture. Japan still had not come out of its cocoon; cultural prejudice was prevalent. Mixed-blood children were looked upon as undesirable people, so I would have many obstacles to overcome and less chance to succeed.

By now, I was so tired of the racial prejudices I encountered during WWII—that is, being called names, spat at, and thrown rocks at as I walked the streets on my way to school and back. Another time, I stood in line for hours and hours to receive food for my family. Then I was told to return to the back of the line if I wanted to take home the allotment for my family. Looking back, I guess that was a lot for a teenager (thirteen to fourteen years old) to encounter on a daily basis. For once, I wanted to be free to speak my mind without watching every word I uttered.

I wanted to make friends with people without wondering if the friendship will last because of some racial prejudice of their parents influencing my friend's decision. Many times, friendships were terminated due to their parents' influence. Some became friendly only for me to find that because post-war Japan was so hungry to learn English, I became their asset or a tool to accomplish their goal.

I was always mindful that people with prejudices were taught to be that way, and we always had a choice to accept or to reject that teaching. My parents taught me ignorant people had problems with prejudices;

only education and social change could bring about positive change. Now over sixty years later, I can see some slow changes. I knew, in my heart, that some day when I least expected it, the ugly head of prejudice would rear its head and hit me again in the chest. That it did, again and again, for at least three more times in my life. Now in my eighties, I learned that the only way to fight prejudice is to educate my children and grandchildren so they can teach others to think the correct way

Rev. L. Grier, a nondenominational missionary came to my town. He and his wife and one small baby boy were assigned to our Presbyterian church. Although he was assigned to our church, he was not bound by the Presbyterian rules and was free to go anywhere to spread the Gospel and even start a new church if he saw fit to do so.

Rev. Grier was a Yale University graduate and his wife was a public health nurse, a baccalaureate-degree nurse with a public health nursing certificate. I felt Mrs. Grier could do a lot for many women of Japan who were in need of sound health information.

I understood that both Griers had six months of intense Japanese language training while in the missionary training school, yet they soon realized that their language skills were far from adequate, and they needed an interpreter to assist them when they got stuck. I was eager to assist them since I was footloose and fancy-free at this time in my life.

Also, I was eager to speak English to someone else other than my parents. My mother had such a thick Southern accent one could cut it with a knife.

First, I accompanied Rev. Grier on a day trip into a small church in the country. I stood next to him and listened to his sermon in Japanese, which he read from the pulpit, and I stepped in to assist only when he would look at me and ask for help. After his sermon ended, he would ask if there were any questions, not only about what he just spoke but also about anything at all. The women would almost always ask about infant nutrition or coping with children's behavioral problems.

Since my mother was a kindergarten teacher and often expanded on child behavior, I knew a little about what to say or add to Rev. Grier's answer. We made a good team. And both of us felt rewarded that we could help in such a manner.

It was around this time that I started to think about what I really wanted to do with my life in the future. If and when I was fortunate enough to be accepted into a university or college in the United States, what would I really want to study?

Both Rev. Grier and his wife encouraged me to apply to several universities in the States. I wrote to Lewis and Clark College with a Presbyterian affiliation in Portland, Oregon. I also wrote to my mother's alma mater, Bessitiff College, and to Mercer University in the state of Georgia. After all the transcripts and necessary red tape were completed, all I had to do was to wait and see.

My parents were both pleased and amazed that I was able to accomplish all the college applications with very little help from either of them. Maybe, I told myself, if I were to choose my own destiny, I must try to do everything myself. I cannot depend on others to help me all the time.

I also sent an application to take the entrance examination for the coeducational section of Doshisha University in Kyoto, Japan.

The examination date was to be in February of 1950. My sister would be taking the same entrance exams too, and both of us started to study and review the books. My sister knew the most recent teaching in Japanese literature, math, and other subjects. She would update me during the year. At times, when I chose to slack off, my sister said things were changing and I was falling behind.

Thanks to her kindness and help, I learned a lot.

Doshisha University

It was a bitter cold February of 1950 when my sister, Anne, and I took the train to Kyoto in order to take our entrance exam for Doshisha University. Our parents had arranged for us to stay with one of their missionary friends, Rev. and Mrs. T.

Rev. and Mrs. T's home was an English-Tudor-style home, with beautiful leaded windows, built by Frank Lloyd Wright in the 1930s. Since Kyoto was not bombed, the house had its original grandeur. As we entered, the entire house had a familiar Western smell. I cannot tell you exactly what it means, but take my word for it, a foreigner's home smells different from Japanese homes.

Anne and I were shown to an upstairs guestroom with a double bed. Chintz curtains framed the window. The bedspread matched the ruffled curtains, and the bed had a gathered skirt around the frame, which matched the window curtains. I had never seen a Western-style bedroom with a matching dresser and nightstands on each side of the bed; even a pair of small lamps on the nightstand matched. The whole room was so beautiful it looked like a page out of a magazine. When my sister and I entered the room, we both looked at each other and said, "Wow, this is so nice."

We unpacked and hurried downstairs for supper. I don't remember what we had for dinner, but whatever it was, it was like going out to a nice American restaurant.

We woke up to a very rainy day with mixture of rain and ice in the streets. Both of us wrapped our warm mufflers around our necks and held our umbrellas close to our bodies so they would not be blown away. When we arrived at the university, we registered and were shown the classrooms we were to go. We were allowed three pencils and one eraser on our desk, nothing else. The pamphlet of instructions and the exam papers were already on our desks. My sister and I sat side by side. For the last time, my eyes made an inspection once around the classroom and looked at the big ugly clock on the wall, then looked outside the window. The cold rain was still beating on the windowpane. I don't remember what subjects were first, but we were tested on Japanese language skills, math, chemistry, history, and English. All of the above subjects were divided into three grueling days of test taking.

When it was all over, my sister and I felt like we were both hit by a nasty flu. All we wanted to do was just go home and rest. Without sticking around to sight see the beautiful old Kyoto, which was saved from being destroyed by the air raids, we thanked Rev. T and his wife and left for home. It took one hour from Kyoto station to Osaka and another hour back to Wakayama. We were so mentally exhausted we hardly spoke to one another. Our parents wanted to know how the exams went, and we told them we thought we did fairly well. I gave credit to my sister for coaching me for the last six months. Many of the subjects and books she told me to review came up in the test, and I was ever so grateful to my sister. I truly think without her help, I might have not passed the entrance exam.

For the next ten long days, we had nothing to do but to wait until the day of posting all the numbers of the students on a large board in the courtyard of the university. The letter of acceptance would arrive later, but if one wanted to know if he or she was accepted, one must go look for his/her assigned number on the board.

My sister and I had a mutual friend who lived in Kyoto, so we decided to ask him to go look for our assigned numbers. Instead of calling us on the phone, he sent a telegram in English. The words were poorly chosen, and we could not tell if one got in or if both of us failed or what. We had no choice but to take the two-hour journey back to Kyoto. I must say we learned a lesson: if you have an important task, do it yourself!

We approached the large display board, and slowly we started to look for our numbers. There they were, like a beautiful picture, our numbers were listed. My sister grabbed my hand, and we jumped up and down, happy that both of us got in. We hugged each other and, when we came to our senses, looked around. There were some students who were crying because they did not make the list. We hurried to a telephone booth and called our parents with the good news. We told them we would be home in two hours. Although we left after breakfast and now it was midafternoon, we were so elated we were not hungry. The only thing in our mind was to get back home and celebrate our good fortune with our parents.

When we arrived home, everyone greeted us with smiling faces and said, "*Omedeto*" (congratulations). That evening, for supper, our nurse who also did the cooking had prepared *sekihan* (a special rice and red bean dish), which is served at each special holiday: birthdays, engagement announcements, weddings, etc.

Now we had just a month before college started in April, and we had to find a place to live and register for our first semester in college.

Geshuku-Sagashi:
to Find a Suitable Boarding House

Most universities in Japan, pre- and post-WWII, had no dormitories. Thus, we thought nothing at all about commuting a long distance to school; most university students commuted up to two or three hours a day. However, we lived too far away. If we were to commute, most of the day would be spent in commuting and hardly any time spent in classrooms or at the school library for research. Remember, personal computers or Internet was not available.

My sister's high school friend had a brother who attended Doshisha University. He offered to ask his brother to look for a suitable boarding house for us. Thanks to my sister's friend's help in Kyoto, we were fortunate to find a very respectable, large private home whose owner was renting several rooms to students. As soon as the message arrived that the lady with the extra room to rent wanted to meet us and have a face-to-face talk, Anne and I went for an interview. Funny, each time we boarded the train to travel to Kyoto through Osaka, the distance we must travel seemed to shrink, and it did not seem so bad a trip.

Both of us were quite excited and curious to find out about the room we were about to rent. What kind of person was she? We heard some stories about unfortunate students trapped in the situation that after the contract was signed and sealed, the disposition of the lady changed from sweet to very unreasonable.

As I remember, Anne and I took a trolleybus after getting off at Kyoto station. The bus took a scenic route right through Kyoto's famous shopping district. Rest assured, we really took note of the location of all of the tall and grand-looking department stores. Remember, our town was bombed and burned to the ground, so the shopping districts had not yet recovered. To see these sights of perfect tall buildings beckoning to two young ladies eager to shop was truly eye candy!

Then the bus stopped in front of Doshisha University, letting off some students. We took note of this location because we would have to travel by bus from our boarding house to the university.

Finally, our destination came, and we found ourselves in a lovely residential area with large Japanese-style homes surrounded by *shirakabe no hei* (white washed mud fences). Most mansions were encircled by these fences to protect the occupants from invaders in the ancient times, but now it was a status symbol of wealth and gracious living. Anne and I walked about two blocks until we came to the house with one of those *shirakabe no hei*, with a big wooden nameplate mounted on the gatepost. Unlike America, there were no house numbers painted at the curb or posted on the house, so people really had to know where they were going.

Anne nudged me and said, "This is the house." With trembling hands, we opened the front door and announced ourselves by saying *konnichiwa* (hello). A lady answered from way back in the house, and soon, a middle-aged neatly dressed woman appeared with a smile on her face. Both of us bowed and said the usual greeting of "*Hajimemashite, dozo yoroshiku onegai itashimasu*" (I'm meeting you for the first time, in good spirits). She answered with another greeting "*kochirakoso*" (same here). Then she told us to come in, motioning with her hand, so we took off our shoes and followed her through a well-polished corridor into a Japanese-style tatami-matted guest room overlooking the beautifully manicured Japanese-style garden. Each rock and lantern was placed proportionately, dotted by bonsai-style miniature pine, maple, and ferns. The garden reminded me somewhat of our own tea garden back in Wakayama, which our mother made next to our teahouse. I felt comfortable here. A few pleasantries were exchanged while we sipped green tea. I think the lady of the house, a widow, was equally intrigued about us: two sisters of mixed blood looking like *gaijin* (foreigners) but speaking perfect Japanese renting a room in her home. I'm certain the story generated plenty of neighborhood gossip.

The upper room

After a while, we were escorted upstairs to a very roomy tatami mat room, with a glassed-in veranda on two sides of the room. The lady said the room next to us was not occupied, but we were to share this corner room, which was adequate for us. I was happy to find a place so nice and yet very private. Now all our bedding, books, lamps, and personal belongings had to be shipped from home. Both Anne and I had never ventured out of our home surroundings, so it was going to be a big adjustment for us and for our parents. Lots of unknowns to face and solve, but that never bothered us. We welcomed challenges. After all, we were young and ready to face the world!

My father used to say, "Until one lives under someone else's roof and eats their food one does not appreciate what one has at home."

I never forgot that saying. My sister and I experienced the typical Kyoto-style cooking, which is called *Shojin ryori*. It is a vegetarian cooking based on the teaching of Buddhism. Because the lady of the house was a devout Buddhist, she cooked mostly with vegetables in season,

134

seaweed, and tofu in all shapes and sizes. Meat, if it were used, was only to season the potato dish called *nikujaga*. I don't remember having some steak or chicken breast at our boarding house. Breakfast was a simple miso soup, Japanese pickles, toasted seaweed, and of course, a bowl of rice. An occasional egg was served, but not often.

All the meals were served downstairs in a large room next to the kitchen. A very large table, enough to seat at least eight to ten people, took up the room.

The very first morning, we found out that we were the only two girls among two young men attending various universities in Kyoto.

Later, we found out one was a medical student attending University of Kyoto from Shimane prefecture, and the other, also from Shimane, was a friend of the medical student, but his interest was not in medicine. Because I left for America within six months after entering college in Japan, I did not get to know them well. However, my sister made lifelong friends with them.

How I Came to USA

Attending Doshisha University in Kyoto was very brief. School started in April and broke for summer vacation beginning August 1. I had my twentieth birthday that summer and went off to attend a Christian work camp to rebuild a road up to the UNESCO (United Nations Educational, Scientific and Cultural Organization) building in Matsue City, Shimane prefecture.

The camp had many Japanese and American students as well as students of other nationalities from all over Japan working together, discussing the Bible, and generally, having a very wonderful time. We talked in Japanese and English with one another and what we wanted to do to rebuild our lives, speculating about our future and sharing our dreams and aspirations.

The physical work using picks and shovels and moving dried clay from the mountainside reminded me of the much younger days when I was forced to help the Japanese military dig a tunnel in the Kimiidera Mountain. However, this time was different; it was for a good cause. Someday we could return and say with pride, "I helped build this road!"

Halfway into our camp work, I received word that I was granted a $500 travel scholarship from the Seven Eastern Colleges Association. This was the word I was waiting to hear. It was music to my ears! In order for a Japanese student to travel to the USA, we first had to have a scholarship from the college we desired to enter, which I had from Lewis and Clark College in Portland, Oregon. Secondly, we needed to get someone to sponsor us for the duration of school. Thirdly, I needed an affidavit from someone stating that he/she would guarantee my fare back to Japan in case of failure to complete college. The word *failure* never entered my mind. I was pretty put out that someone would think that I might fail! But that was the rule, and our Rev. Grier kindly wrote a note of guarantee needed to satisfy the American consulate in Tokyo. Mid-August, I was ordered to come to the American consulate for an interview and to prepare to receive my student visa.

The interview was pleasant, but the consul general made it clear that I was allowed only to study, I must not work for money, I must not get married while in school, and the visa was only good for four years. He made me swear that I would adhere to these rules.

My passage to the USA was purchased on the cruise ship SS *President Cleveland*. Later, I found out that this ship was used for troop transport of American soldiers during WWII. There were no commercial aircraft flying from Japan to the United States. It was only five years past the surrender and the economy was just beginning to recover. MacArthur's American occupation army was still stationed all over Japan. We were still under occupation.

Lewis and Clarke College began in early September, and my ship was to sail September 5, 1950. I would be late to school, but I didn't care. I was going to America!

I stayed in Tokyo with my sister for a few days to receive all my inoculations for travel. I had to go to St. Luke's Hospital to receive typhoid, cholera, and smallpox vaccinations. Next, I had to get a chest X-ray to prove I was free of tuberculosis. When all this was over, I was pretty exhausted and feverish. My sister had to nurse me while I stayed another day in the hotel room to rest; I could not move. Then we went back to Wakayama.

The day came for me, with one footlocker and a red suitcase, to depart Japan for the land of my dreams, America, my mother's homeland, and the college in Oregon.

One of the worst typhoons hit Japan the day I left Wakayama to go to Yokohama. In the pouring rain, I had to board the ship. My mother and sister accompanied me to the harbor. The wind was blowing very hard; white caps and choppy big swells prevented the ship from docking. The ship was anchored midway in the harbor. The dream of throwing colorful ribbons from the ship to the loved ones on the dock was shattered. I accepted my fate of never having a chance to throw the ribbons we had so happily purchased. The ship was anchored quite a way from the dock, and now we must get in the small tender boat to get to the *President Cleveland*.

I looked at my mother and sister and hugged and kissed each good-bye. They had tears in their eyes as I did. Mother made certain that I had all my documents: passport, visa, tickets for the ship, for the bus from San Francisco to Portland, Oregon, the names, addresses, and phone numbers of my sponsors, etc.

The time came to step into the small tender boat, which was rocking up and down.

I was wearing a dress and new saddle shoes, which I had purchased for this trip, and it was difficult to step down in the boat. Now that I was in the small tender being carried away to the big ship, I looked back through the small window of the boat, but I could not see my family. I looked to see if I could see Mt. Fuji, but it was shrouded with dark storm clouds. I did not even get to say good-bye to Mt. Fuji, usually shining with its white peak above the wispy clouds. Although I was upset, I told myself that the images and memories would sustain me for whatever I faced in the future.

When we were assisted onto the ship and told to register at the main deck, I thought I was in some beautiful palace with newly refurbished accessories on the walls. The carpet was so thick my shoes seemed to sink as I walked up to the desk. I soon forgot about the scary trip from the dock to the ship where everyone was hanging on to their seats with white knuckles.

The registration was quite simple. The purser, who was quite pleasant, spoke English, and I understood everything he said. When that was done, I was shown the stairs down to the foreign students' quarters, three decks down. We passed the students' dining hall, which was lined with picnic tables and benches, and then we came to the men's dorm, then the men's and women's showers and bathrooms.

All the girls were ushered into a large room, without windows, lit with wall lamps. They must have had six rows of bunk beds with each unit three beds high, lined wall to wall. There was only a small space to pass through the units. I was shown the bunk bed closest to the floor and was very happy that I did not have to climb up and down those narrow ladders. I put my suitcase under the bed in the space that I had to share with two other Chinese-speaking students who came behind me.

Soon, the dorm was filled. There were no other Japanese students on this ship. I was the only one.

Lots of rich Chinese were sending their children to schools in America. I could tell they were wealthy by the Chinese silk dresses they wore. They were all slender and beautiful and spoke Chinese mostly among themselves, but when I had a question to ask, they spoke to me in perfect English.

Top Row   Lillian Natsue————— ↓

All the foreign students on board the *President Cleveland*

The large ship bobbed up and down in the ocean like a toy boat. It also rocked side to side, which caused the dishes to slide. We had to hold onto our plates so they would stay safely in front of us. I ate my dinner but could not keep it down for long. Soon, I was running to the WC to give it all back to the fishes. I was sick for the entire twelve days until we reached Hawaii (Honolulu) and another few days to San Fransisco disembarkation. I lost ten pounds, all my clothing hung on me. I had to take a tuck in my waistband to keep my skirt from slipping off when I walked.

One Portuguese purser took pity on me and brought water and food to my bunk and told me to eat even though I had to throw it up. That is when I realized someone was keeping an eye on me so I would not fade away. We docked in Honolulu for one day to bring aboard passengers and provisions.

I remember well when the same Portuguese purser asked me if I was getting off at Hawaii. I said that I was afraid that I would lose my way and would be unable to get back on the ship. He laughed and said, "I'll take you around Hawaii and make certain you get back to the ship."

I was naive and trusting. Fortunately, the purser must have taken pity and showed me around Honolulu. We walked through the park, looked in the shops, and ate some mango and papaya. This was my first experience walking alone with a man and being treated to exotic tropical fruit, looking at the palm trees and all the beautiful sweet-smelling flowers. I was feeling much better, no more upset stomach. Though my body was still swaying with the ship, this tropical paradise agreed with me, and I wished that we could stay on the island a little bit longer.

After Hawaii, the ocean was much calmer, and the severe rocking of the ship stopped. I was so glad that whatever I ate did not come up. I felt much better, and now I could challenge any problem that came my way.

The captain announced that we were approaching the Golden Gate and anyone wishing to see the famous bridge should be on the main deck. All of us students scrambled up three flights to the deck to see the Golden Gate.

Fortunately, the weather was clear, and the morning sun was dancing on the water as though it was welcoming me to America. Soon, the bridge loomed around the bend, and as we watched, we went under the bridge. It was so huge and long; I have never seen such a sight.

Another announcement came over the speaker directing us to gather all our belongings and come to the debarkation deck. As we crossed the ramp to the pier, there was all our checked baggage waiting for pickup.

Third-class passengers, we students, made a long line to clear customs.

I was to be met by a Presbyterian mission person at the pier and to be taken to the Presbyterian Church Mission in Chinatown to spend the night so I could board the bus for Oregon the next day. I must have waited for two hours. The customs officers were long gone, and there was hardly anyone left at the pier. I asked an old lady cleaning the pier where I could find a phone. She pointed to the next large open area and told me to put a dime in and then dial. I said, "Excuse me, what is a dime?" I knew the denominations of the coins, but I never heard that ten cents was a dime. I had some change, so I produced several twenty-five cent pieces and some ten cent pieces. She pointed to the dime in the palm of my hand and said, "This is the dime you want." I thanked her and went over to the phone, put the dime in the slot and dialed the number. When I said, "I am still waiting on the dock and no one has picked me up," the voice on the other end said, "A person was sent to the dock to pick up a Japanese girl, but she came back stating she could not find you." Then and there I realized they were looking for a pure Japanese girl with long straight black hair. I told her that I was half white and half Oriental with light brown, curly hair and that I did not look Japanese at first glance. The person on the phone instructed me to stay right where I was and they would send another person right away. In about half an hour, a smiling young Chinese girl appeared and greeted me with apologies.

I felt very relieved, safely in someone's care, on my way to a hot meal and a nice clean bed for a good night's sleep without the rocking sensation of the ship.

The next morning, after breakfast, the kind people took me to the bus station. I found out I had missed the early-morning bus. The next one was leaving in the afternoon. I had about four hours to kill, which I did not mind. Just then, a young Japanese-looking man came up to me and said, "Don't I know you from the *President Cleveland*?" I looked at him and recognized that he boarded the ship in Honolulu on his way to Eugene, Oregon. He attended the University of Oregon and was going to be a junior this year. We exchanged greetings.

The young man said, "My friend, who came to see me off, has a car, and since we have some time to kill until we have to be back here to board the bus for Oregon, why don't you come with us?" I thought that was a splendid idea. The drive took us through Golden Gate Park and on the coast. We stopped at the Cliff House, a restaurant built on a huge rock with the waves crashing against it. It was a spectacular view. It was somewhat early to eat lunch, but since we had to get back to the bus station, the young men suggested going to a taco stand on the beach just down from the Cliff House. I thought, *Tako. That's wonderful. Tako*, in Japanese, is *octopus*. How nice it was that Americans also liked octopus. When we reached the taco stand, I still didn't realize what taco was. I had never tasted Mexican food in my life. I stood behind the young men while they ordered, so I did not see what it was until they handed me the taco.

My eyes opened wide when I looked at this unusual item. I said, "This is not tako. I don't see any tentacles in this food." The young men started to laugh so loud they almost spilled their drinks in the sand. They soon realized I meant octopus. Hawaiians ate octopus too, so they realized I had never had a taco before, and this was my first experience.

The joke was on me. After I was told they meant Mexican taco and not octopus, we all had another laugh. I learned another word that day. The taco was very delicious.

The trip was a long one on the Greyhound bus, about twelve hours or more, because the bus stopped at various large towns to let off or pick up passengers. I remember we stopped at least six times, with one stop an hour break for dinner at the coffee shop in the depot. I ordered a hot turkey sandwich, thinking it was some turkey with two pieces of bread. When it was placed in front of me, it was turkey on bread, covered with gravy, mashed potatoes, and peas. It was a royal banquet for me. After all, I just had one taco at lunch before boarding the bus.

The bus took us through the mountains on very curvy roads, with tall trees on both sides of the two-lane highway. I started to get the same queasy feeling I experienced on the ship. Soon, we came to a flat valley, and my stomach stopped giving me trouble.

The young student, going to Eugene, Oregon, sat next to me and pointed out and explained some of the historical spots as we passed. The landscape changed constantly, fallen trees, not cut up or taken away for firewood. I thought, *What a waste.* I came through a war-torn Japan where wood was precious, and every bit of wood was used for firewood if not for something else. I could not get used to the wide expanses of space with nothing, no buildings, no animals, not even a stray dog. I was used to crowds, people, and cramped quarters. These wide open spaces seemed a waste. Strange, after a while, I got used to it and felt relaxed and calm, dozed off and took a nap.

The young friend got off at Eugene, Oregon, and said good-bye. He said he hoped to see me again when he visited his friend in Portland. We exchanged addresses and phone numbers. After that, he kept his word and came to see me at my sponsor's home one more time before he graduated and went back to Hawaii.

The bus rolled into Portland though it was late. My sponsor, Dr. B, was waiting at home when I called. He said he would be at the bus depot in about forty minutes. He lived in Beaverton, which was a way out of town, and it took a while to get into town. The music was loud inside the bus depot. The "Tennessee Waltz" was playing. This was the first Western music I was exposed to. Now every time I hear the song, it brings back memories of the Greyhound bus depot in Portland.

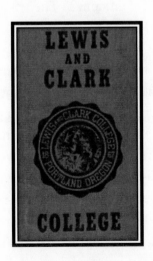

Lewis and Clark College
and Nurses Training

Dr. B took a few hours from his work at the VA Hospital in Vancouver, Washington and took me to school at Lewis and Clark College on the east side of the Willamette River on Palatine Hill. The college is in a beautiful setting with old mansions on the grounds. We passed the gatekeeper's house at the entrance and went to the foreign student advisor's office. Dr. B told me that I must depend on the bus to take me home when school was over that day.

The foreign student advisor was a short middle-aged woman with a soft kind voice. She helped me register for my classes, eighteen units of difficult subjects: physiology and anatomy with lab, chemistry with lab, English I, and PE. She showed me my locker and said, "Your classes started two weeks ago, so you are going to have a tough time catching up." Since I did not know how behind I was, it did not bother me. She then pointed to a building and said, "I'll show you the commons." I asked myself, "What is a commons?" The answer didn't come until I entered the building, and much to my surprise, it was a cafeteria. The advisor seated me at the table and treated me to a soda and told me I could attend the afternoon class of physiology/anatomy.

I was at my class early and introduced myself to Professor B. The lady professor was well dressed in a suit with her golden hair in a French twist at the back of her head. She looked very professional, dressed in a gray suit. She graduated from some Eastern university and was teaching physiology, anatomy, and biology to premed students. Since I majored in nursing, my courses were all mapped out for the next four years. The professor told me to take a seat and told me that, unfortunately, this was a test day and I need not panic but put down what I knew. Professor B gave a mini test every two weeks, and just my luck, I had to take a test I knew nothing about.

It was a one-page test, naming bones in the arm and hand—ulna and radius in the arm and parts of the bones in the hand.

I knew some of the names partially in Japanese, but not in English. I understood the question and wrote the answer in Japanese. The test was collected and passed on to the teacher. The lecture started, and she spoke so fast that even though I understood it all, I was unable to take notes in English. I quickly translated what she said into Japanese and wrote profusely. When it came to the name of bones, I wrote in *romaji* (write as it sounds using the English alphabet).

When the day was over at 4:00 p.m., I had to take the Palatine Hill bus, which stopped at the college, down the hill to the Terwilliger bus station, then transfer to another bus leaving for Beaverton. All in all, it took two and one-half hours to get back to my sponsor's home. That day was sheer exhaustion. After supper, I fell into bed and slept to the next morning at 5:00 a.m. when the alarm woke me up.

I had physiology/anatomy three days a week with the lab class; I got to know Professor B pretty well. She told me when she looked at my first test paper, she laughed out loud. She could not read kanji, so she could not give a grade on my first test, but she would give me a chance to make it up if I took the test in English later.

SEVEN OF THE NEW STUDENTS FROM FOREIGN COUNTRIES. Front row from Left: Reinhard von Ammon, Germany; Lillian Euhara, Japan; Ingebjorg Sverklie, Norway; Werner Wilkening, Germany. Back row: Toshiko Makino, Kimiko Hamada and Kenneth Iga, of Japan.

I squeaked by the first semester with C grades and one D. The D was in English because of the Japanese Jinglish, a coined word of my husband. To this day I cannot shake the Jinglish. My sponsor said since I was trying very hard, they would consider it as an adjustment period. Even American students had a difficult time on their first semester. I knew I had to make all Cs or better to pass. I stayed up until 2:00 a.m. studying each night and got up at 5:00 a.m. to get dressed, eat breakfast, and take the bus back to school. I did not waste time on the bus; I read the chapter of lessons for that day and was prepared to ask questions.

I also memorized all 206 bones in the human body, this time in English so I could pass the test. Please don't ask me to recite the same now as I'm certain I would flunk.

I thank God that I had two and a half hours of bus ride each way so I could review for the test I was about to take. The second semester was still difficult, but I passed with C grades. At least the first year of college came to an end with passing grades. All prenursing students had to take premed classes and continue college through the summer. I had only a few days off between the end of the regular school and when summer school began.

My sponsor's wife was a pediatric nurse and had worked at a hospital in Boston before she married the doctor. She was a very efficient manager and ran her home like a hospital. She had a two-year-old son and one on the way. She was having a difficult pregnancy, which kept her in the house during the day. She was only to get up to come to the table for dinner. Most of the time, she was on the couch in a horizontal position.

When I came back from college, I would see to it that the washing and ironing were done and dinner was on the stove. She would tell me how to cook. I had never cooked prior to this time. This was a real awakening. However, I enjoyed the work and took care of the little boy, bathing him and tucking him into bed. Soon, the pregnancy came to term and Mrs. B had a baby girl. The baby was an experience I never ever dreamed of having. The laundry stacked up, so I had to wash every day. In 1950, we hung clothes out on the line and there were no disposable diapers, so all had to be washed and hung to dry. The work at my sponsor's house after school took more time. I felt my chores never ended until almost 10:00 p.m. I would go to bed and set my alarm clock for 2:00 a.m., get up, and study until 4:00 a.m., then sleep for an hour to get up at 5:00 a.m. or so. This went on for at least another year until I entered the nursing phase of my practicum and had to stay at the Emanuel Hospital Nursing Students Dormitory.

I felt I was reprieved from hard labor. For the first time in my life, I now experienced dorm life, having a roommate and making lifelong friends.

When the second year was over my grades were As and Bs with one C (English, what else). I did well in the nursing practicum and made all As. I enjoyed the pharmacology classes and had no difficulty memorizing long names of medications. Japanese schooling was mostly memorization, so learning medical terms, diseases, instruments, and equipment came easy for me. Other young nursing students were struggling to memorize Latin names of diseases.

Chemistry was easy my first year as it was a review of my course in high school. I was not familiar with the chart of atomic weights. Japan used the metric system, so I had no problem with measurements in chemistry and pharmacology.

By the end of the second semester the original fourteen students majoring in nursing dropped down to eight. The dropouts said "it was too difficult."

At the end of my first year, I met with my foreign student advisor, and she told me that my scholarship would continue because I was a foreign student. However, the college expected me to make a B average after the second year. My goal was set, so I continued to study hard. I was determined to make the grade and continue in my chosen profession. By now, I was getting used to taking notes in English.

After my second year was over, I met with my foreign student advisor and discovered that my scholarship was given by the Boyd Coffee Company in Portland, Oregon. They produced commercial coffee and coffee-brewing equipment. I remembered purchasing several cups of Boyd coffee on my way back from school at the bus depot. I decided to write a thank-you note and make an appointment to see the person who was so kind to present me with the funds.

The day came for the appointment to meet the founder and director of the company. I was dressed in my only red suit brought from Japan, with hat, gloves, and high-heeled shoes. I looked pretty spiffy. I took the correct bus and arrived at the coffee company office and announced myself to the receptionist. The reception room wall was decorated with the company logo and many factory photographs. A potted ficus tree was placed in the corner. The carpet was very plush, and when I walked, my heels sunk in deep. I sat with my white-gloved hands folded carefully on my lap, making certain my knees were together and poised in a position so that I could stand at a moment's notice.

Soon, the secretary for Mr. Boyd came out and motioned me to come into a large mahogany-paneled room. Mr. Boyd, a gray-haired tall gentleman, was seated behind an enormous desk. He looked at me and got up, extended his hand, and shook my hand gently while saying he was very glad to see me. He asked me about my background, schooling, and my major. I showed him my transcript and thanked him for his support. He smiled and said he had sent scholarships to many students in the past, but I was the first one to make the effort to come to see him and thank him in person. He told me not to worry, that my scholarship was assured for the next two years. When I left his office, I was given a pound of coffee for my sponsors. As I walked away, I felt like I was walking on air; my worries for financial support were over, and I could concentrate on my studies from now on.

By the beginning of my second year, we were starting the curriculum for nursing. That summer, the whole class moved into Emanuel Hospital Nursing Students Dormitory. This was my first experience in a dormitory and having a roommate. My roommate was a tall brown-eyed, brown-haired, soft-spoken young lady. She was very kind and considerate. Her parents would often invite both of us to their apartment in Portland, and I would enjoy a weekend of wonderful hospitality. Her mother, Mrs. P, was from a German ancestry and cooked the most delicious sauerbraten in the world. Her sauerkraut would melt in your mouth. Mrs. P would always send cookies back with us when the weekend was over and we had to return to the dormitory.

On special occasions Mrs. P would hand me a $5 bill or, at times, $10, saying, "Here is something to tide you over." For me, five dollars was like "It's manna from heaven." Remember, foreign students were prohibited from working for money, and General McArthur prohibited the Japanese yen from being exchanged into dollars to be sent out of Japan. I was at the mercy of my kind sponsors to give me cash ($20/ month) for my school supplies, bus fare, and for my personal use.

Five dollars in 1950 purchased a very nice pair of shoes or a lady's hat. A pair of nylon stockings cost between seventy-five cents and a dollar. So Mrs. P's gift to me meant I could occasionally buy a nice blouse or a sweater to keep warm. I really learned how to manage money wisely.

Emanuel Hospital School of Nursing was a well-known excellent school of nursing in Portland. The teaching staff was strict but kind and had patience for the young girls in probation called probies. We wore the probies' uniform, which was blue and white checked with a white Peter Pan collar. The hospital emblem patch was on the right sleeve. We wore a white starched apron, without a bib, on top of the uniform.

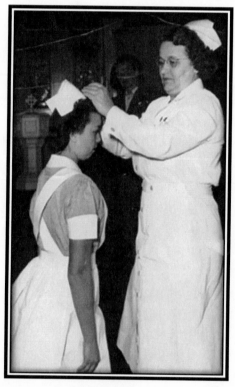

Capping ceremony

When we passed probation and received the nursing school's cap at the capping ceremony, we were allowed to attach the white bib to the apron.

I remember we would all line up for morning inspection with our caps placed just right, our uniform clean without soiled spots, and our shoes polished white. We had to show our hands, nails trimmed flush with the end of the finger, no nail polish of any kind. If any of these points were in violation, you were sent back to your room to correct them and received demerits and denied off-campus time after hours.

After all, I had reminded myself of the promise I made with the American consul general back in Japan that I was to be in the USA for the purpose of education and not to make boyfriends. I did not have to worry, like most girls in my nursing class, about having a date and returning after curfew only to find the dorm's doors locked. When that happened, they had to call their roommates from outside the dorm so they could sneak down the stairs past the housemother's room to open the front door and let them into the dormitory. This kind of sneaking around was very dangerous. When caught by the house mother, usually a white-haired widowed lady with keen sense of hearing, could mean demerits, which translated to being grounded.

Being bilingual was handy and interesting. One day, while I was a student nurse, the head nurse on the medical floor called me to her station and told me there was a patient just taken off a Russian ship that came into the port of Portland. He apparently had a severe heart problem and was on bed rest; that meant that the patient was ordered to stay in bed and not allowed to get up, go to the bathroom, or take a shower. Everything must be done for him, including using the urinal or bedpan in bed. No matter how the nurses explained in English, he just ignored that order. The head nurse found out that he spoke Japanese, so she asked me to talk with him and see if he could be convinced to stay in bed.

When I walked into the room, he took one look at me, smiled, and said in perfect Japanese, "You are half Japanese, aren't you?" I'm certain he looked at my name tag that said Lillian Uehara, Student Nurse. I was surprised that his Japanese was so perfect without the usual foreigner's accent.

I asked him where he learned such perfect Japanese. He told me that during the Japanese occupation of Manchuria, he was working for the Mantetsu (a Manchurian railroad for the Japanese government), and he was forced to learn the language in order to work as an engineer. After a few pleasantries, I explained that his heart condition was such that he must be on absolute bed rest. He promised me that he now understood and would not try to get out of bed.

The next day, the head nurse was very pleased that he was a perfect patient and thanked me for talking to him. From this experience, I learned that two-way communication was vital in our lives, especially between patient and caregiver. I experienced it firsthand and never forgot what I learned, especially that active listening was so important when one was trying to obtain information vital to the patient's recovery.

Lillian visited by Anne 1952

The three-year nursing curriculum was packed into two years. That meant we did not have the luxury of a spring or summer vacation. My pediatric affiliation started in the summer of my third year at University of Oregon Medical School, Doernbecher Pediatric Unit in Portland. The next affiliation was at the State of Oregon Psychiatric Hospital in Salem,

Oregon, and the next affiliation was back to the State TB Sanitarium in Portland. The third year flew past me like a dream. I enjoyed moving every three months to the different affiliations, learning the particulars of each unit of my assignment. The months flew before I was back to Lewis and Clark College for my fourth year, taking upper division required courses to graduate from college. I made good grades, and my parents and sponsors were happy with my progress. The final hurdle was to take the Oregon State Board of Nursing examination. All my nursing classmates took the exam together, and thank goodness, we all passed.

Later, Professor B, my biology professor and the nursing program director, told me that she was very happy that I came through with flying colors. Looking back to the first day of our meeting, she told me she really worried how I was going to overcome all the obstacles in my path. This program is difficult even for an American-born student, let alone a foreign student coming from a vastly different educational system.

The cap and gown was worn with pride on the day of graduation from Lewis and Clark College. Now I had to worry about getting my student immigration status changed to permanent resident so I could get more experience under my belt before I returned to Japan.

Around 1954, there was a severe shortage of registered nurses in the United States. When I visited the U.S. Immigration Office in Portland to inquire about changing my status, I was very surprised that they said yes. Immediately, the immigration officer told me to get a certificate of employment from a hospital, and I could stay as long as I wished.

Since I trained there, Emanuel Hospital offered to employ me. I observed firsthand that when student nurses continued to work at the same hospital, they received their training, they continued to be treated like students. If one goes to a different hospital, one is respected as a new graduate. So I chose to work at Good Samaritan Hospital in Portland and was able to obtain a certificate of employment, which the immigration office required. I chose to work in the large operating room earning $250/month as an OR Nurse. I was there several years until I was asked by a physician to be his office nurse.

Office Nurse for Dr. S

Dr. S was a general practitioner who was a resident physician at Emanuel Hospital when I was still a student nurse and happened to know me through his wife whom I had the pleasure to care for as a patient. She liked my bedside manner and thought I would make an excellent office nurse. Mrs. S told her husband to find me to be his office nurse when he was ready to open his practice. So you see, new experiences kept falling into my lap.

By the end of my second year as an OR nurse, I had considerable knowledge on how to set up and scrub (scrub nurse) for many different types of surgeries, including heart and chest. The medication for tuberculosis patients was not as sophisticated as today, and most patients ended up with a lobectomy, losing one side of their lung.

Later, this operating room experience became a lifesaver at Dr. S's office. One day, a patient came into the office with a severely gashed finger, not enough to seek emergency care at the hospital, but the laceration was deep enough to require stitches.

When we asked the patient if he was allergic to Novocain or any other "cain" drugs, he told us no. We then proceeded to give him the Novocain by injecting around the site of the injury and started to sew his finger. The procedure was halfway through when the patient complained of a fainting feeling, with cold sweats and nausea—textbook-perfect signs and symptoms of beginning anaphylaxis. This is where my OR training was the factor in assisting the physician in bringing the patient out of that state of shock.

Even for a very minor surgery, before the physician came into the room to start the actual procedure, I was trained to have the oxygen tank, mask, and proper tubing ready for use. The tank valve was cracked open and ready. A vial of adrenaline and Benadryl, a few syringes, appropriate needles, and tourniquet for intravenous or subcutaneous injections were ready for use. I was prepared for any immediate need.

With one look at the patient, I knew he was in trouble, and so were we. His blood pressure kept dropping, and he started to shake and sweat. I said one word, *anaphylaxis*, and placed the oxygen mask on the patient's face and told him to breathe deeply. Fortunately, the patient was still responding, and I asked the doctor which method of injection he wanted to use. He told me and we were successful at bringing the patient back to a safe state. It happened so quickly that had I not prepared for the worst, it might have ended in a disaster.

I was calm, cool, and collected until it was over. After that ordeal, my legs felt like rubber. Both the doctor and I were thankful we were prepared. Dr. S used to tease me about all the preparation I went through even for a very minor suturing procedure, but he never teased me again and thanked me profusely for the foresight and training I had which saved this patient. Consequently, my next month's paycheck showed a raise.

I will never forget this experience as long as I live, and to this day, it is so vivid in my mind. I feel like it just happened.

The Saga of House Arrest

Of many comical experiences during my late nursing years, three episodes stand out among my memories. The stage is set during early 1978 through 1980 before I became a supervising public health nurse and, later, the director for the Home Health Agency for the County of Orange, California.

A nurse with a bachelor's degree and additional training for public health nursing receives a public health nursing certificate.

When I was in the master's degree program at Loma Linda University School of Graduate Nursing, I was in my late forties and had a much better concept of public health nursing than the young nurses in their twenties just out of college with no nursing experience.

The work of a public health nurse is guided by a referral passed to the field nurse by the district supervising nurse. A referral is written or phoned from any physician, public or private, hospital staff, social service, or law enforcement and is sent to the district office of the public health supervising nurse. Each referral is prioritized and recorded, then assigned to a specific field nursing staff.

The purpose for the visit is clearly written. Therefore, the public health nurse visiting the patient in his/her home environment will explain the reason for the home visit. The nurse is instructed to assess the patient and the home condition, teach, and document the visit so the physician can determine the next step in helping the patient. We are extended eyes, hands, and ears for the referring source. Heavy responsibility is on our shoulders to make accurate assessment and reports.

One day, I received a written referral from a physician stating a diabetic senior citizen had a very badly swollen leg and had an infection, which required changing dressings each day. The caregiver was his wife with questionable mental status. After she was shown how to change the wound at the hospital, they never kept the return appointment for a recheck. Two weeks had passed and the physician was concerned about the patient's leg wound.

It was a nice summer day and I was glad to get out of the office that morning. When I reached the row of apartments, I promptly spotted the apartment, where the patient resided. They lived behind a large swimming pool. I had telephoned the wife before I visited, so she was expecting me. I walked up to the front door and knocked. Soon, it opened and a fairly well-groomed middle-aged lady answered the door. When I introduced myself and handed her my official name card, she compared it with the name badge on my blouse, then nodded and motioned for me to come inside. The apartment was clean and neat. Her husband, surprisingly much older than she in his late sixties and somewhat obese, sat in a reclining chair with very swollen legs, dangling. I did the usual temperature, blood pressure check, and listened to his heart. I then asked to see his medication and asked him how he generally felt. He told me his leg was much worse, and it pained him deep inside his leg.

All this time, his wife gave me a watchful eye. When I told him I must take the bandage off to see the wound, his wife seemed agitated and told me she had just changed the dressing today and I did not have to do it again because he complained of so much pain when she changed the dressing. I listened empathetically but, this time, asked the patient directly if I can take the bandage off and look at the wound. *He gave his consent.* I put on my sterile gloves and proceeded to take off the dressing. I could see the wound was badly infected and his lower limb was so tight from swelling; it had split open beyond the actual wound with blood and pus oozing. Some parts of the leg were showing the beginning signs of gangrene. I carefully turned to his wife and said, "This wound is worse than I expected to see, and you must take him back to the physician as soon as possible for further treatment. If you do not, he might lose his leg."

She looked at me with hostile eyes and, with a very loud voice, told me, "You can't tell me what to do. I know how to care for my husband,

and by the way, you are under house arrest. I'm going to call the cops." With that unexpected announcement, she went to the phone and called 911. Then she said, "The cops are coming. You better not leave."

During my orientation period, we were told such things can happen, but now it was happening to me. I quickly dressed the wound and stood up to gather my equipment and waited for the police to arrive. Soon, with siren blaring, came two officers. When they came to the door, the wife told the officers I was hurting her husband, and she kept yelling, "Put the cuffs on her, put the cuffs on now." The officers were so taken aback, one stood next to her and the other came up to me smiling. I explained the situation and presented my credentials with the physician's referral. They took one look at my nursing badge, and the officer near me told me to follow him outside while she was still shrieking "put the cuffs on."

Outside, the officer told me that they had some previous calls from this apartment, and they felt the wife had a mental health problem, to say the least. The officer escorted me to my parked car and told me it was good that I stayed until they arrived. It is against the law to run away while one is under house arrest. Needless to say, I did not make any more house calls that day. I had enough surprises.

My nursing director heard the story, called me to her office, and told me she was proud of my conduct during the episode. Still smiling, she told me that for over twenty years, she has served the public, but this was the first time any of her nurses was put on house arrest. We all laughed.

My district supervisor called the physician and told him the problem with his patient's leg. When he heard what happened to me during my home visit, he apologized profusely and said, "Please convey my apology to that nurse." The patient was hospitalized again, but this time, his leg was amputated.

Man with a Gun

All field nurses were trained in infant assessment. This meant going into the home to assess the mother-and-child interaction and to complete a physical examination of the mother and infant.

The region I was serving was well-known as an ongoing drug trading area and was under constant surveillance by the police department. Many times, we would detect drug dealing in the streets or around the home we were to visit. In such cases, we were told to come back to the office and report to the physician why we were excused from completing the referral. We were never asked to put our safety in jeopardy. With keen observation skills hammered into our brain, we were always mindful of our surroundings.

One day, I was requested to visit the home of a drug-abusing mother and her infant. I telephoned the home to make an appointment. The teenaged mother answered the phone and told me she was glad a nurse was coming to visit her. She said the baby was crying all the time and he was "driving her up the wall." I felt fairly comfortable with the situation like this due to my extensive training. I was also much older than the young nurses just out of college without much real-life experience. To these young inexperienced mothers, I looked like their aunt or mother, and they would often open their hearts to me.

The neighborhood was in the rough part of town. Houses were in disrepair with trash piled in the streets and stray dogs wandering around. I noticed an unmarked car parked on the street with two men in it watching the neighborhood. I had a gut feeling that they were police officers from the drug surveillance department. As I was looking for a place to park, one man showed his face out of the car window and asked me what I was doing in this neighborhood. When I told them and showed my county ID, they said, "OK, you can go in the house." I parked my car and walked up to a dilapidated house and knocked on the screen door. A young man answered the door and told me they were expecting me. As I entered halfway into the home, I noticed a black gun in his left hand halfway behind his back. I said with a calm voice, "Please put that gun away. I'm a public health nurse who is only interested in the welfare of your wife and baby." He nonchalantly looked at the gun in his hand and said, "Oh, I'm sorry," and promptly put his gun away. He told me later that he always answered the door with a gun in his hand because they were afraid some drug-crazed person might come to the door.

As I walked farther into the front room I noticed a marijuana plant growing under a special light on the side table in plain view. The house had a distinctive smell like someone had just finished smoking a joint. When I asked, they told me, without hesitation, that both of them just finished a joint before I came to calm their nerves.

After some simple yes and no questions, I proceeded to examine the infant on the kitchen table. Everything went well as a first-time home visit should go. There was a lot of teaching to do beginning with how to swaddle an irritable infant who sadly inherited his mother's drug habits and now was having a rough time trying to kick the habit all alone.

I taught how one should not jostle the infant up and down like most mothers do. Rather, they should swaddle the infant and calmly hold the infant and rock side to side so not to irritate its brain stem. As I demonstrated how to swaddle and calm the infant, just like magic, the crying baby calmed down and promptly went to sleep. The demonstration was successful, and I was able to gain their confidence. There were many more visits with a happy ending. The mother and son "kicked the habit" together as I closed the case six months later. I only hoped that their life would be a better one in the future. Thank my lucky stars I never had to face a person with a gun again.

The Encounter with a Mouse

The orientation program for a newly employed public health field nurse included a six-month probation period. During this time, the supervisor accompanied the nurse on several field visits to teach and observe the level of her nursing skills. After I became a supervising public health nurse, I always enjoyed a joint visit with my new nurse. It brought back memories of the good old days.

The county I served originally was packed with orange groves. Even though some of the groves were replaced with housing projects, they often had problems with field mice invasion. Vector Control was quite busy at times.

It was a nice spring afternoon when Ms. T and I set out on a joint visit to a postpartum early-discharged mother and infant. Early discharge from the hospital meant that the patient is discharged one day after delivery and many problems of the postpartum period were just starting to manifest themselves. Although this case was an early discharge, the mother had three other small children and did not seem to suffer from any problems.

We always taught the new nurses not to sit on a couch or an overstuffed chair. Make certain you sit on a wooden or plastic covered chair to protect yourself from sitting in a wet place where children often had accidents with their bladder control or spilled their red Kool-Aid.

Ms. T was mindful of that warning and sat next to the kitchen table and proceeded with her home visit. This nurse grew up in a rather affluent family and had never seen a cockroach climbing up the wall or a mouse running around the house in broad daylight.

Ms. T was through with her infant examination and was in the middle of taking the blood pressure of the mother sitting on the couch.

The nurse had just placed the blood pressure cuff on the mother's arm and was leaning toward her with her stethoscope in her hand. The nurse heard some scratching sound, and out came a cute gray mouse with black beady eyes from under the couch, stopped in its track, and gazed at Ms. T. When Ms. T saw the mouse eye to eye, she screamed and jumped up on the wooden chair like a pole vault athlete. It happened so fast it was almost comical.

With the blood pressure cuff still on the patient's arm and the rubber bulb dangling from her arm, the young mother never changed her facial expression and said, "We do have some problems with rodents coming inside the house." I looked at my nurse and told her to get off the chair. The mouse is more scared of us than you are of him. Her face was flushed, and she started saying, "But, but." I finally told her to calm herself down and proceed to do what she came to do.

By this time, all the children had stopped running around and were in the living room, laughing at the nurse who was scared to see a single little mouse. We did some simple questioning and found that this neighborhood of low-income housing was infested with cockroaches and field mice. Thanks to the gray creature, we did some hygiene teaching and referred the whole neighborhood to Vector Control.

Ms. T was still shaking when she left the apartment. I thought she would quit on the spot and never come back, but she stuck it out. We still correspond at Christmastime, and I enjoy teasing her about her probation days of trials and tribulations.

To be continued

Edwards Brothers, Inc.
Thorofare, NJ USA
September 13, 2011